# Day Paddling
# Long Island
# Sound

# Day Paddling Long Island Sound

Eben Oldmixon

THE COUNTRYMAN PRESS
WOODSTOCK, VERMONT

With time, access points may change, and signs and landmarks referred to in this book may be altered. If you find that such changes have occurred at the sites described in this book, please let the author and the publisher know so that corrections may be made in future editions. The author and publisher also welcome other comments and suggestions. Address all correspondence to:
Editor
The Countryman Press
P.O. Box 748
Woodstock, VT 05091

ISBN 978-0-88150-684-6

Book design and composition by Faith Hague Book Design
Maps by Paul Woodward, © The Countryman Press
Cover and interior photographs by the author

Published by The Countryman Press, P.O. Box 748,
Woodstock, Vermont 05091

Distributed by W.W. Norton & Company, Inc.,
500 Fifth Avenue, New York, NY 10110

Printed in the United States of America

10 9 8 7 6 5 4 3 2 1

# Acknowledgments

*T*HE AUTHOR extends thanks to Dr. Michael Retsky for being invited along on trips in his big double to look at the Norwalk and Bridgeport areas and for information on the facilities and attractions there.

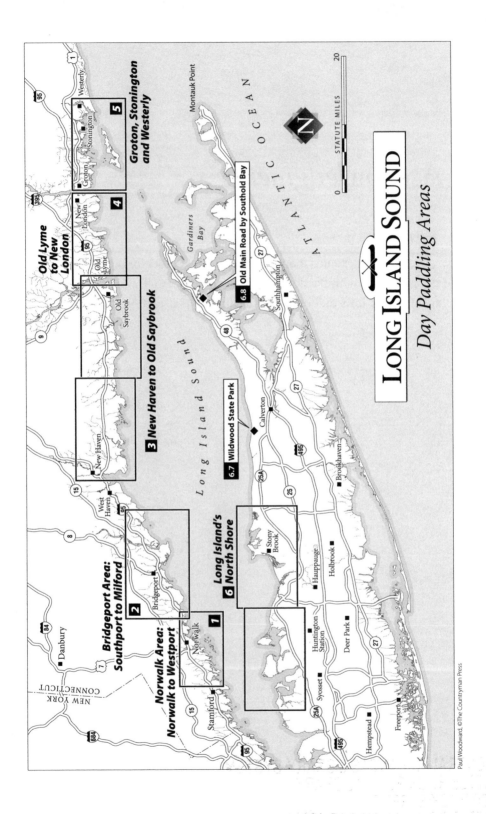

# LONG ISLAND SOUND

*Day Paddling Areas*

**1** Norwalk Area: Norwalk to Westport

**2** Bridgeport Area: Southport to Milford

**3** New Haven to Old Saybrook

**4** Old Lyme to New London

**5** Groton, Stonington and Westerly

**6** Long Island's North Shore

6.7 Wildwood State Park

6.8 Old Main Road by Southold Bay

STATUTE MILES

0    20

N

NEW YORK
CONNECTICUT

Danbury
Stamford
Norwalk
Westport
Bridgeport
West Haven
New Haven
Old Saybrook
Old Lyme
New London
Groton
Stonington
Westerly

Hempstead
Freeport
Syosset
Deer Park
Huntington Station
Hauppauge
Holbrook
Stony Brook
Brookhaven
Calverton
Southampton
Montauk Point

*Long Island Sound*

Gardiners Bay

ATLANTIC OCEAN

CTCAG = Connecticut Coastal Access
Guide
ConnYak = Connecticut Sea Kayakers

# Contents

# Introduction

## Shoreline Access

Long Island Sound measures somewhat more than 110 miles from Mount Vernon, New York to the mouth of the Pawcatuck River in Rhode Island, if we stretch our definition of Long Island Sound in the east to include Fishers Island Sound and Little Narragansett Bay. At its broadest, between East Haven, Connecticut and Wildwood State Park on Long Island, it is 20 miles across, but along most of its length it is less than 15 miles in width, and typically one can see from shore to shore.

Its western two-thirds is sheltered from the swells of the Atlantic under most conditions: there are many days in summer when it appears to be a large tame lake.

The Connecticut shore is crinkly, and if the 70 miles or so from Stamford east to Stonington could be stretched straight, there might be half again that distance, maybe more, of coastline bordering the sound. The same can be said for the western 50 miles of the north side of Long Island, and there are 30 miles of straight beach east of that, out to Orient Point. The New York mainland may add 15 or 20 miles more. We might guess that that a walking tour along the tide line of the sound would be over 230 miles long.

No wonder that so many kayakers and canoeists fervently wish to dip a paddle in its waters.

To say that the shores of Long Island Sound are densely populated and highly valued barely begins to state the case, however. The western two-thirds of the Connecticut and north Long Island shores have probably reached the terminal stage of utilization: almost every inch is spoken for and occupied, and not only occupied but declared off-limits to any but its owners or at most local residents. The situation eases in Connecticut the farther east one goes, and as a rule Connecticut makes access easier than does Long Island, but still, a paddler driving in from another town or state cannot expect to stumble easily upon places to launch into the sound.

This book is intended to help paddlers find access points that they may not have known about and to inform them about pleasant places to see, once out on the water, while staying free from run-ins with others users of the sound, for if the Long Island Sound shoreline is crowded, the sound itself near a harbor can be like the entrance to an active hive of bees as powerboats buzz in and out.

# Web Information About Public Shoreline Access for Cartop Boaters

## Connecticut

The State of Connecticut's Department of Environmental Protection and the University of Connecticut maintain the Connecticut Coastal Access Guide on the Web; go to www.lisrc.uconn.edu/coastal access or www.dep.state.ct.us/coastalaccess. Click on "Boating Search" (currently in a panel along the left-hand side) and in the screens that come up look for little silhouettes of boats on trailers and boats on top of cars. This site shows evidence of being the product of considerable effort, thought, and energy, and it is valuable as a starting point or as a way to refresh your memory about resources available along a part of the Connecticut coastline you may be thinking of visiting. It considers the banks of the main rivers entering the Sound, even fairly far upstream, to fall under the "coastal access" rubric, which this book does not, and so paddlers can find out about, for example, the Had-lyme Ferry Boat Launch, 11 miles up the Connecticut River from its mouth. Not all the available kayak launching locations are covered in this site's listings, and not all the sites listed as being available for cartop boat launching are really suitable for pleasant, low-risk access to the waters of the Sound: additional research may be needed, such as that involved in preparing this book. Even with this caveat, however, Connecticut is to be praised for its coverage of coastal access resources and even more so for the series of state-maintained boat launching ramps along its shoreline.

ConnYak, one of the kayaking clubs in Connecticut, provides another reference resource. The club maintains a Web site with information about some of the members' favorite launching spots: www .connyak.org. ConnYak at present shares, quite generously, information about 31 launching sites on the Sound's shoreline, up various Connecticut rivers, and farther east on Narragansett Bay in Rhode Island.

## New York

No equivalent resources have been found listing launching sites for kayaks along the North Shore of Long Island.

A group called Long Island Paddlers (www.lipaddlers.org) maintains a Web site with links to useful information on tides, for example, but at present the section called "Launching Sites" has entry restricted to Long Island Paddlers members only.

One may peruse a New York State road atlas such as DeLorme's *New York State Atlas & Gazetteer* and jot down the locations of the boat launch symbols along the north side of Long Island, then meander along the coast. However not every symbol will turn out to be associated with a place where a kayaker from out of town can park and launch, nor would one always feel comfortable launching a kayak from all the locations indicated. Nevertheless, there are several state parks open to the general public with water access, and several town-maintained ramps with an associated stretch of flats where a kayaker would feel perfectly at home.

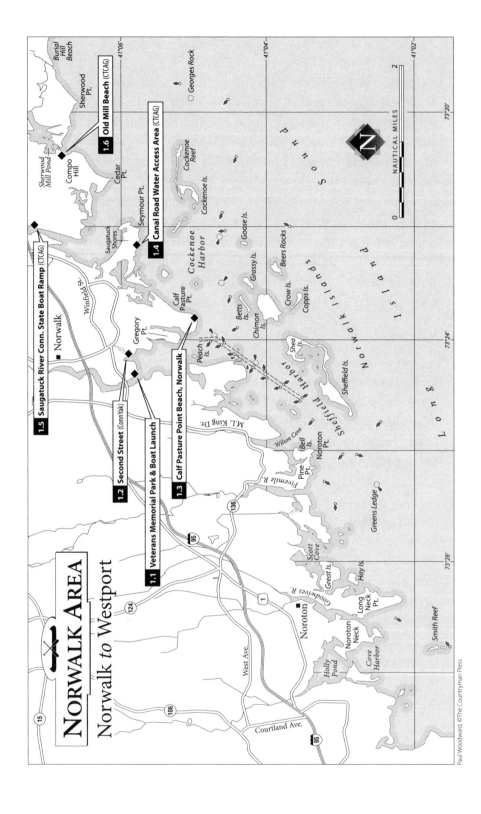

NORWALK AREA
*Norwalk to Westport*

1.1 Veterans Memorial Park & Boat Launch

1.2 Second Street (Conn'Yak)

1.3 Calf Pasture Point Beach, Norwalk

1.4 Canal Road Water Access Area (CTCAG)

1.5 Saugatuck River Conn. State Boat Ramp (CTCAG)

1.6 Old Mill Beach (CTCAG)

Burial Hill Beach

Sherwood Pt.

Sherwood Mill Pond

Compo Hill

Cedar Pt.

Seymour Pt.

Saugatuck Shores

Winfield St.

Norwalk

Gregory Pt.

Calf Pasture Pt.

Cockenoe Harbor

Cockenoe Reef

Cockenoe Is.

Georges Rock

Goose Is.

Grassy Is.

Beers Rocks

Crow Is.

Copps Is.

Betts Is.

Chimon Is.

Peach Is.

Shea Is.

Sheffield Harbor

Sheffield Is.

Norwalk Islands

Long Island Sound

Sound

M.L. King Dr.

Wilson Cove

Bell Is.

Pine Pt.

Noroton Pt.

Fivemile R.

Greens Ledge

Scott Cove

Great Is.

Hay Is.

Goodwives R.

Noroton

Long Neck Pt.

Noroton Neck

Cove Harbor

Holly Pond

West Ave.

Courtland Ave.

Smith Reef

124

95

136

1

106

95

15

NAUTICAL MILES
0        1        2

73°28'    73°24'    73°20'

41°06'    41°04'    41°02'

Paul Woodward, ©The Countryman Press

# CHAPTER 1
# Norwalk Area:
# Norwalk to Westport

NORWALK AND WESTPORT are exceptionally friendly to cartop boaters, for kayakers and canoeists are offered access to Long Island Sound at several fine launching sites. From any of these places, paddlers can easily reach the Norwalk Islands to enjoy an archipelago close to 5 nautical miles (nmi) long from end to end, with low scenic islets that appear peaceful and unspoiled. Ruddy turnstones and oystercatchers feed along the quiet stretches of their shores. (See Fig. 1.)

*Fig. 1.* *The south side of one of the smaller Norwalk Islands. Birds gather densely on the soundward sides of these islands to nest, recuperate, and feed. Gulls and cormorants are visible in this picture, but common and least terns are present, too.*

West along the coast from Norwalk in the direction of Stamford there are miles of deeply indented shores and the outlets of the Five Mile and Goodwives Rivers, which are engaging to explore. These can be reached by paddlers who begin from, say, the public park in Norwalk. That would make a pleasant day trip out and back; it is about 6 nmi from Norwalk's park to the mouth of the Goodwives River.

Sad to report, little shore access is granted free of charge to out-of-towners near these rivers: one beach in Darien was charging $40 for parking. Within and east of Norwalk, $15 or so seems to be the norm, but a paddler can avoid even that cost by starting from other locations. In many towns along Connecticut's shore, access is provided free of charge at the state-maintained launching ramps, indicated on road signs by the symbol of a trailered boat on a wedge.

This is the case shoreward of the Norwalk Islands: the Saugatuck River descends through Westport, the town east of Norwalk, and beneath the I-95 highway bridge crossing the Saugatuck River is a

*Fig. 2. Veterans Memorial Park in Norwalk, Connecticut. Kayakers and canoeists arriving back in Norwalk toward the latter part of the day may be able to take their boats out at the "visitors' dock" at the northern part of the park's waterfront along the Norwalk River. This can be useful if the tide is low and the southern end of the park is too muddy.*

Connecticut state boat ramp. Many kayakers will find it congenial to start their Norwalk trips from here.

Veterans Memorial Park in downtown Norwalk also offers free access to the water, here, of course, on the Norwalk River. (See Fig. 2.)

Second Avenue, a short distance farther south along the east bank of the Norwalk River from the park, ends in a small, informal access area.

All three of these launching sites provide recreational kayakers with excellent starting points from which to reach the Norwalk Islands.

The Norwalk Islands are worth repeated visits. They probably are near the top of many paddlers' lists of the friendliest and most scenic destinations in Long Island Sound.

Paddlers should study a nautical chart that shows the entrance to Norwalk Harbor in some detail before venturing out; the intersection of powerboat traffic from four directions ought to be avoided. (See Fig. 3.) I say "four" because although there is no marked channel between

***Fig. 3.*** *Looking north into the Norwalk River from its mouth. This view greets paddlers returning from a day out among the Norwalk Islands. Veterans Memorial Park is straight ahead. However, powerboats converge on the area of the river's mouth in the near middle distance from ahead, from behind, and from the left and right. One way to reduce encounters with them is to go to the right and cross a single channel to get close to Calf Pasture Point before entering the river.*

Shea and Chimon Islands, outboards do come through that gap in quite a hurry before they reach the speed restriction zone.

One suggested tactic is to hug Gregory Point and then Calf Pasture Point, continuing around in front of that shoreline until the chimney visible on small Betts Island is due south, 180° magnetic (m) from your boat, then paddle toward it; be alert for traffic, for the north side of the channel is not marked at this point. Green can #9, however, marks its other side, and the channel is barely 200 yards across. Another tactic is to paddle from Calf Pasture Point to Cockenoe Island (sight on the pole on the island: 97°m, reciprocal 277°m; distance 1.7 nmi). The eastern channel still has to be crossed, but that is described below.

Cockenoe Island at the east end of the group offers a bit of wildness, especially out by Cockenoe Reef. Paddling south off the end of the reef puts you over Cockenoe Shoal, with scattered, barely submerged rocks; observe that there are three buoys: a green to the east, a red to the south, and a red to the west, which separate paddlers from traffic on the Sound.

**Fig. 4.** *The length of Long Island Sound stretches out beyond a stony shore on one of the Norwalk Islands.*

The two red buoys south of Cockenoe Shoal are the first two in a series marking the eastern channel into Norwalk Harbor. Paddlers will spend the least time in this busy channel if they take up a position by red nun #4 at the west end of Cockenoe Island, by Channel Rock, and then go directly over to green gong #5, 0.3 nmi to the west, close to Goose Island.

No marked channel goes between the remainder of the islands—Goose, Grassy, Beers, Chimon, Copps, Crow, Shea, and Sheffield—to name the main ones. Along and off their shores, waterfowl and shorebirds carry on their daily business. Remember the guiding principle of interacting with them: "Do not cause an animal to alter its behavior." (See Fig. 4.)

Not only wildlife can be found in among the islands; on occasion a sailing ship takes up anchorage, and it can appear startlingly large against the scenery of sandbars, shells, and grass. (See Fig. 5.)

**Fig. 5.** *A three-master has maneuvered into a snug anchorage in the narrow strait between two of the western Norwalk Islands. This vessel is active in studies of the ecological health of Long Island Sound.*

There is a lighthouse from the Civil War era on the west end of Sheffield Island, an interesting structure that appears more like a town hall or a church (see Fig. 6), and on the north side of the island there are docks and other landing places where paddlers can pull in for a

**Fig. 6.** *This lighthouse, now decommissioned, dates from the time of the Civil War. It faces west down Long Island Sound toward New York City and is a massive presence at the west end of Sheffield Island, the westernmost of the Norwalk Islands.*

visit. The western half of Sheffield Island and all of Chimon and Goose Islands are in the Stewart B. McKinney National Wildlife Refuge, so fortunately, at least these portions of the Norwalk Islands can be expected to remain largely unchanged for the future.

The water north of Sheffield Island is called Sheffield Harbor, and the second channel into Norwalk Harbor runs down its midline, marked by closely spaced pairs of buoys. If you are paddling back up into Norwalk, consider crossing this channel west of the mouth of the Norwalk River, before you encounter traffic associated with the eastern channel as well. Be aware, though, that the western channel does hug the point of land at the west side of the Norwalk River mouth very closely.

Incidentally, the west side of the Norwalk River, south of the built-up waterfront, has in places a remarkably oozy bottom, loose unpacked silt that is neither liquid nor solid; at low tide a kayak can find itself stuck on top of the flats made of this peculiar material, and if the boat cannot be rocked and paddled free, then getting out to push can be awkward. Keep a hand on the perimeter line around your boat, for the ooze is deep and will not support your weight, and wear tough-soled shoes, too, for there are thousands of sharp oyster shells in there. Their edges gouge troughs in wood, fiberglass, epoxy, and plastic—almost anything a small boat might be made of.

Back over on the east side of Calf Pasture Point there is an embayment with Sprite Island in the middle and Saugatuck Shores and Seymour Point as its eastern arm. This is a pleasant shore to paddle along, too, with a little canal and beaches large and small.

East of the peninsula that ends in Seymour Point and Bluff Point is the mouth of the Saugatuck River, whose mouth is 0.65 nmi wide; the other side of its mouth is formed by Cedar Point and Compo Beach. The Saugatuck is popular with paddlers, even those who do not wish to go out to the islands, for it offers at least 3 nmi of calm paddling, attractive views of the small town of Westport, and a current that is almost always negligible. What is more, 1.5 nmi upstream from Bluff Point is the Saugatuck River state boat ramp, the premier launching site for kayakers in the Norwalk area.

If one day, when starting from the Saugatuck River, you would like to see some of the coast instead of the Norwalk Islands, it is entirely possible to head east. East of Cedar Point, back at the mouth of the Saugatuck, the coastline is formed into a series of gentle scoops, perhaps half a dozen, depending on how you count them, in the 3.5 nmi to Southport Harbor and the 6 or 7 nmi to Bridgeport. The 3-fathom line tends to lie 0.2 nmi or farther from this shore, and under most conditions this area should offer pleasant paddling for sea kayaks.

From the Saugatuck River boat ramp to the Black Rock Harbor launch site in Bridgeport is about 10 nmi by water, if one cuts from point to point along the way. With a kayak that cruises at 3 knots, with attention to the tidal currents and the winds, and with the logistics about how the boats are to be picked up worked out, this would be a scenic midlevel alongshore outing.

## Launching Sites

Note: "CTCAG" after the site name means that a description of the launching site may be found online in the Connecticut Coastal Access Guide. "ConnYak" after the site name means that ConnYak (Connecticut Sea Kayakers) has a brief description of the site on their Web site at www.connyak.org/.

# 1.1   Veterans Memorial Park and Boat Launch (CTCAG)

*Address/Location/Appearance*

Seaview Avenue, Norwalk, CT; 41°05'47"N, 73°24'38"W. (See Fig. 2.)

*Getting There, Parking, and Fees*

Consult the Connecticut Coastal Access Guide for driving directions. Route 136 crosses the Norwalk River in the center of Norwalk. On the eastern bank of the river, perhaps a hundred yards from the bridge, Seaview Avenue branches southeast off Route 136, and the entrance to the park is to the south almost immediately after the vee. Drive south beside the riverbank until the roadway begins to curve left where it nears the end of the point of land, and park. There are usually free spaces near the launching site, but other parking spaces can be found a short walk away.

There seems to be no charge for using the park to launch canoes and kayaks away from the powerboat ramps.

*Launching*

Launch boats straight ahead through the marsh grass. This is convenient only several hours to either side of low tide.

You pass a parking lot and ramp for trailered boats on your right as you come in. Kayak launching from the ramp is discouraged, but toward evening, when things have slowed down, it seems to be acceptable to recover your boat there. This could be handy if the tide happened to be low when you arrived back in Norwalk.

### On the Water

See comments on the best ways to reach the Norwalk Islands elsewhere in this chapter. Usually the best plan is to keep to the east side of the river until you round Calf Pasture Point to avoid the intersecting powerboat traffic lanes.

# 1.2   Second Street (ConnYak)

### Address/Location/Appearance

Second Street, Norwalk, CT; 41°05'45.0"N, 73°24'14.2"W. (See Fig. 7.)

**Fig. 7.** *The foot of Second Street, Norwalk, Connecticut. This small launching site is tucked between two buildings and easily overlooked from the water, but offers a firm beach and a location convenient both to the Norwalk River and the Islands.*

### Getting There, Parking, and Fees

Consult the ConnYak Web site for driving directions. Where Route 136 runs north–south for a short distance in East Norwalk, it is part of East Avenue. Continue south beyond where Route 136 bends west towards Norwalk and look for a small cemetery on the left; turn left at the south end of the cemetery and then make a quick right onto Gregory Boulevard. Follow Gregory Boulevard to a traffic light; go through the light and make a right onto the first street after the light; this is Second Street. Go to the end of the street. There is a little beach here, rather stony, and there is usually parking to be found on the surrounding streets.

If it is more convenient, Second Street can also be reached by coming along Seaview Avenue from where it branches off Route 136 at the east end of the bridge across the Norwalk River. After Seaview Avenue passes the end of the mill pond and the intersection with East Avenue, it bends left to become First Street. Turn right on a side street (New Street, for example) and at the end of the block turn right onto Second Street.

## Launching

The bottom here is firm enough to allow boats to be launched and recovered at low tide, but there is a powerboat channel dredged out to a depth of 6 feet immediately off the beach. Take the usual precautions.

## On the Water

After launching, look back at the beach to see what you will be searching for on your return, for this is a snug little location and tends to lose itself between the buildings.

If you are going out to the eastern islands, consider keeping to the east side of the river until you reach a place alongside Calf Pasture Point where you can hold 135°m (reciprocal 315°m) for 0.75 nmi to red flasher #8; from there it is a quick skip 0.2 nmi due south (180°m, reciprocal 0°m) to the east end of Grassy Island across the channel.

If you are going to the western islands, consider turning due west (270°m) at Gregory Point to make it across the main channel in about 100 yards.

# 1.3    Calf Pasture Point Beach, Norwalk, CT

### Address/Location/Appearance

Calf Pasture Road, Norwalk, CT; 41°05'11.7"N, 73°23'35.4"W. (See Fig. 8.)

**Fig. 8.** *Calf Pasture Beach, Norwalk, Connecticut. On one hand, out-of-towners pay to park; on the other hand, the Norwalk Islands are close by.*

### Getting There, Parking, and Fees

Consult the driving directions for the Second Street site for directions to Gregory Boulevard, which ends on Gregory Point farther south. Gregory Boulevard is crossed by Third and Fifth Streets; take either street one block to the left and turn right; Third Street meets Ludlow Manor, which then crosses Marvin Street (the extension of Fifth Street) to become Calf Pasture Beach Road; turning right at Fifth Street (Marvin Street) brings you to Calf Pasture Beach Road on the right. Drive to the end. There is plenty of parking.

Parking for Norwalk residents costs $5; nonresidents park for $20 on weekends, less at other times.

### Launching

Launching is often easier from this sandy beach than from the muddy bottom upriver. Another advantage is the lovely view from a broad sandy beach and the somewhat shorter paddling distance out to Chimon Island.

### On the Water

Consider the comments in this chapter on how to get out to the islands with the least exposure to powerboat traffic. Head east to explore the small cove. Round Seymour and Bluff Points and go over to Compo Beach. Poke along the other side of that peninsula as far as Old Mill Beach.

# 1.4  *Canal Road Water Access Area (CTCAG)*

### Address/Location/Appearance

Canal Road and Cockenoe Drive, Westport, CT; 41°06'01.5"N, 73°22'41.3"W. (See Fig. 9.)

**Fig. 9.** *Canal Road and Cockenoe Drive, Westport, Connecticut. The Canal Road site offers somewhat limited parking, but a fine view, plus a perfect starting location for paddling out to the Norwalk Islands and exploring farther eastward along the shore.*

### Getting There, Parking, and Fees

The launching site is at the intersection of Canal Road and Cockenoe Drive in Westport, on the west side of the peninsula.

From either west or east, take exit 16 off I-95 and come south on East Avenue. Drive south on East Avenue about 0.4 mile to the intersection with Old Saugatuck Road (this is also Route 136 for a short distance). Turn left onto Old Saugatuck Road and follow it about 0.9 mile to where Harbor Road and Minard Drive come in from the right, before a sweeping curve to the left. (Old Saugatuck Road becomes Duck Pond Road in this vicinity.) Turn right onto Minard Drive and immediately bear left onto Harbor Road.

Follow Harbor Road alongside the water for 0.7 mile; then turn right to follow Canal Road across the peninsula for 0.2 mile. The launching beach is straight ahead at the end, and parking is on the landward side of the street, in the angle of the turn.

There is space for about four cars. No fee is charged.

## Launching

The bottom here is firm, and one may launch at any tide.

## On the Water

There is no channel between the end of the peninsula on which Saugatuck Shores sits and Cockenoe Island, which lies 0.75 nmi on a bearing of 160°m from Seymour Point, the end of the peninsula; the waters are in fact less than 3 feet deep in most places at mean low tide.

Heading west back along the peninsula brings you to an opening into an enclosed, shallow, calm salt pond to the east fringed with docks and waterways that wind through marshes to the west.

# 1.5 *Saugatuck River Connecticut State Boat Ramp* (CTCAG)

*Address/Location/Appearance*

Saugatuck River Connecticut State Boat Ramp, Westport, CT; 41°07'12.04"N, 73°22'01.91"W. (See Fig. 10.)

**Fig. 10.** *Saugatuck River State Boat Launch. Two paddlers set out from the premier launching site in the Norwalk area for paddlers to see what a day out on Long Island Sound will bring.*

*Getting There, Parking, and Fees*

The boat ramp is on the east bank of the Saugatuck River almost directly underneath I-95 where it crosses the river, but you get there by driving on secondary roads.

See the Connecticut Coastal Access Guide on the Web for driving directions from I-95 in either direction. The trick is that there are three access roads to the boat ramp, one of which may be closed. One

(Elaine Road) goes west off South Compo Road south of the I-95 overpass and north of the railroad bridge, which are quite close together. The others (Saxon Lane closer to the river and Underhill Parkway some 150 yards farther east) go south off Route 136 before it crosses the Saugatuck River into Westport; coming across the small bridge on Bridge Street from Westport's shopping district, look for Saxon Lane and work your way down toward the river and underneath I-95. Underhill Parkway joins Saxon Lane on the north side of I-95, before crossing underneath to the launching site. In either case, whether driving along Route 136 or South Compo Road, watch for the characteristic state boat ramp signs.

### Launching

The ramp is well maintained, but its surface can be slippery with algae; wear shoes with nonskid soles.

### On the Water

There are no exceptional cautions to be observed. Downstream toward the mouth of the Saugatuck there is a marked navigational channel for powerboats, about in the middle of the river mouth, and there may be many small sailboats on the water.

*The placid Saugatuck River upstream from the State Boat Ramp. Paddlers cross in front of the Westport riverfront and will go under the small bridge to enter the upper reaches of the river, a popular local paddling destination.*

# 1.6   Old Mill Beach (CTCAG)

## Address/Location/Appearance

Old Mill Road, Westport, CT; 41°06'42.0"N, 73°20'49.4"W. (See Fig. 11.)

**Fig. 11.** *The beach at Old Mill Road, Westport, Connecticut.*

## Getting There, Parking, and Fees

From either east or west on I-95, take exit 18. Go north on the Sherwood Island Connector about 0.25 mile to the intersection with Greens Farm Road; turn left (west) onto Greens Farm Road. Greens Farm Road turns south-southwest; follow it to close to I-95, where it intersects with Hills Point Road. Turn left onto Hills Point Road and follow it south past Sherwood Millpond on the left. Immediately after the millpond dam, Old Mill Road goes off to the left; turn in and after 20 feet or so bear right into the beach parking lot.

Parking in the Old Mill Beach lot is adequate for two or three dozen cars. However, use is restricted to Westport residents from Memorial Day to Labor Day.

No fees are charged out of season.

## Launching

This area has a sandy bottom, and launching is possible at any tide.

## On the Water

Out to a line just inland of one connecting the points of land to east and west (Sherwood Point and Cedar Point) the embayment is shallow. Beyond that the bottom slopes off quite steeply and conditions approach those out in the Sound—the area being quite exposed to the east and southeast.

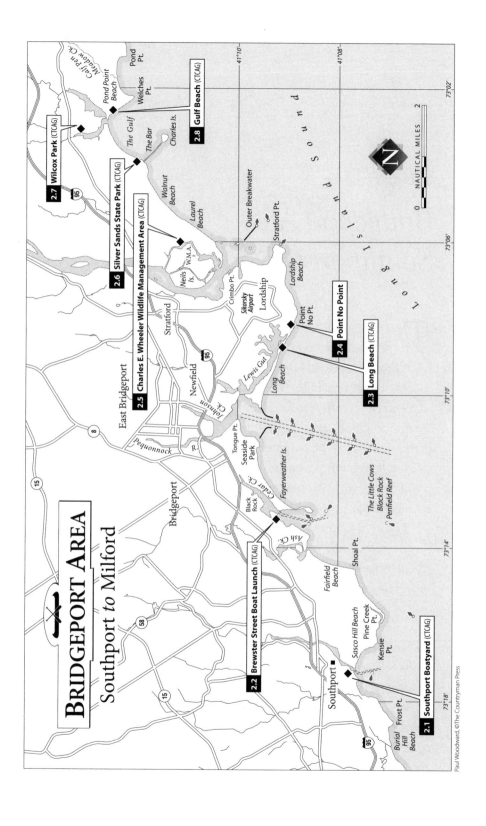

# BRIDGEPORT AREA
## Southport to Milford

Paul Woodward, ©The Countryman Press

**2.7 Wilcox Park** (CTCAG)

**2.6 Silver Sands State Park** (CTCAG)

**2.8 Gulf Beach** (CTCAG)

**2.5 Charles E. Wheeler Wildlife Management Area** (CTCAG)

**2.4 Point No Point**

**2.3 Long Beach** (CTCAG)

**2.2 Brewster Street Boat Launch** (CTCAG)

**2.1 Southport Boatyard** (CTCAG)

Long Island Sound

NAUTICAL MILES

0    1    2

Pond Pt.

Welches Pt.

Pond Point Beach

The Gulf

The Bar

Charles Is.

Calf Pen Meadow Ck.

Walnut Beach

Laurel Beach

Neil's W.M.A.

Crimbo Pt.

Outer Breakwater

Stratford Pt.

Lordship Beach

Lordship

Point No Pt.

Sikorsky Airport

Stratford

East Bridgeport

Newfield

Pequonnock R.

Bridgeport

Black Rock

Lewis Gut

Johnson Ck.

Tongue Pt.

Seaside Park

Fayerweather Is.

Cedar Ck.

Ash Ck.

Long Beach

The Little Cows

Black Rock

Penfield Reef

Shoal Pt.

Fairfield Beach

Sasco Hill Beach

Pine Creek Pt.

Kensie Pt.

Southport

Frost Pt.

Burial Hill Beach

41°10'

41°08'

73°02'

73°06'

73°10'

73°14'

73°18'

95

8

15

58

15

95

# CHAPTER 2
# Bridgeport Area: Southport to Milford

*T*HE BRIDGEPORT AREA described in this chapter extends from Southport on the west side of the city to Milford on the east, a span of roughly 14 nautical miles (nmi). Bridgeport itself, in the middle, is not particularly attractive to kayakers and canoeists, because it is a waterfront city with heavy shipping and ferry traffic moving within the harbor and along the entrance channel. However, to either side there are small welcoming harbors and beaches, off of which you can paddle a bayworthy kayak while viewing coastal scenery and experiencing the real personality of the Sound.

The area is interrupted also by the outflow of the Housatonic River, which, while frequented by powerboaters, is too powerful near its entrance into the Sound to be included in this book of easy to moderate paddles: we cross the river's mouth here, but do not venture inside.

Kayakers have been known to strike out from Bridgeport and cross the Sound to Port Jefferson, New York and back, paralleling the course of the big ferries, but this is another feat not included in this book.

Instead, we point out that there are Southport Harbor, Black Rock Harbor, The Gulf, and Milford Harbor to play in, and if one is comfortable paddling up to a mile offshore, it is quite possible to paddle coastwise point-to-point from, say, Black Rock Harbor to Milford Harbor, rounding Fayerweather Island, Point No Point, Stratford

Point, and Charles Island on the way. This day trip covers 11 nmi, or somewhat more.

Let us examine that route in more detail. Launch into Cedar Creek at the end of Brewster Street and cross at once to the east side of the channel. Paddle south along the west side of Fayerweather Island to its end, where there is an abandoned lighthouse. (See Fig. 12.)

*Fig. 12. Fayerweather Island, Bridgeport, Connecticut. After launching from the Brewster Street ramp, this is the view a paddler sees coming up to the end of Fayerweather Island's peninsula. The lighthouse is abandoned, but wading shorebirds and seabirds congregate at the point to feed in the shallows.*

Red beacon #2A, surrounded by riprap, lies off the point, and you could paddle out to it, but just as much enjoyment may be had by hugging the point just closely enough to see what the shorebirds are up to on the beach and in the boulder-rich shallows.

After that, you check your equipment, take a deep breath, and set out for Point No Point, which is 3.9 nmi away on a heading of 98° magnetic (m) (reciprocal: 278°m). As you plan to start from flashing red #2A and wish to make landfall on Point No Point, you shave the heading to 96°m (reciprocal: 276°m). Then you remember that you are going to be crossing the Bridgeport Harbor Entrance Channel, with the big boats traversing back and forth to Port Jefferson on Long

Island at least twice an hour. You want to know precisely where you are in relation to the channel, to be able to see whether any ferries or other boats or ships are coming, and to get across the channel in the shortest possible time.

The pair of channel markers closest to your course is flashing green #9 and red nun #8, just offshore of where your straight-line course would take you, and you decide to make the point-to-point traverse in two segments, holding up beside green #9 before crossing briskly to the inshore side of red #8 and then proceeding to Point No Point. You shave the heading a little more, to 94°m for a distance of 1.55 nmi. Holding up a little way from the flasher, you will make certain that nothing whatsoever is approaching from either direction, and when you are sure, you will scamper 150 yards across the channel, leaving red nun #8 on your right.

*One of the large, fast ferries that travels back and forth between Bridgeport, Connecticut, and Port Washington on Long Island leaving the mouth of Bridgeport Harbor. It is possible to cross the ferry route safely and paddle between launching sites east and west of Bridgeport, but preparation and alertness are required.*

As part of your just-in-case planning, you make a mental note that from your jumping-off point by Fayerweather Island to about half the way to green #9, the shortest distance to shore is back along the way you came. At about two-thirds of the way along that leg, the entire beach between Fayerweather and Seaside Park on the west side of the harbor entrance is essentially equidistant. However, once at green #9, the closest land is at Seaside Park. Once on the east side of the channel, since the shore west of Point No Point is straight, the shortest distance to shore is always along a course of 45°m.

Tucked into your things-to-avoid category is a note that a heading of 82°m from the tip of Fayerweather will carry you to the beacon at the end of the breakwater guarding the east side of the Bridgeport Harbor mouth, which would be a questionable place for a paddlecraft, so you resolve to keep your course south of 82°m until you are perhaps better than halfway to green #9.

If instead of paddling directly from Fayerweather Island to Point No Point you follow the shoreline of the Bridgeport Harbor Bight, you pass several launching sites described on the Connecticut DEP Web site: in Bridgeport, Park Avenue and Newfield Avenue; and in Stratford, Long Beach. From the tip of Fayerweather Island to a spot on Long Beach where the isthmus is narrowest, paddle 3.1 nmi on a course of 90°m; you cross the Bridgeport Harbor Entrance Channel at buoy pair red nun #10/green can #11, 1.2 nmi from the beach. This route takes you up to 0.75 nmi from shore between Fayerweather Island and the buoys; again, Seaside Park at the west side of the harbor mouth is the closest landfall.

From your position on the east side of the channel beside red #8 to a landfall on Point No Point is 2.4 nmi on a heading of 98°m. You recall that you may be able to get a sandwich in a restaurant at Point No Point, which, as its name implies, is hardly any point at all. (See Fig. 13.) The landing site there is a short beach with a small rock jetty at its eastern end. Behind it is a blocky building with a restaurant on the first floor; its understanding staff has been known to tolerate the slight dampness that may accompany even careful kayakers stopping in for fuel.

Back on the water, you see that moving east from Lordship Beach 0.9 nmi brings your boat to the end of Stratford Point and a view of the mouth of the Housatonic River, which is not an inconsiderable stream. On the far side, about 0.45 nmi away bearing approximately 55°m, is a rock jetty lit at its southern end with red flasher #2A. You could head just south of that landmark, but there often is rough water

***Fig. 13.*** *Point No Point, Stratford, Connecticut. Here it is possible to park, launch, land, and lunch at the same beach.*

off the end of the breakwater, especially when the river outflow collides with the tidal current and waves off the Sound. This patch of chop could be irregular and rough enough at times to inconvenience some boats and paddlers, and so it might be prudent to avoid it. The chart shows a green buoy #1 with a green flasher (2.5 sec) and a bell, bearing approximately 75°m, at a distance of about 0.5 nmi from the easternmost part of Stratford Point. As that buoy is about 0.2 nmi out beyond the end of the jetty and the rough water should have settled down at this point, you plan that leg of your trip.

The next leg could take you to the southern tip of Charles Island, which is 2.6 nmi from green #1 on a course of 56°m, but that takes you 1.1 nmi from the nearest land, and you foresee that you may want to be close to the shore at that time of day and with that many miles behind you.

The alternative seems to be heading straight for the entrance to Milford Harbor; that would make a leg 3.75 nmi long at a heading of 45°m. The chart shows, however, that that leg would cross The Bar, a connector between the mainland and Charles Island exposed at low tide and probably awash when you reach it. Fortunately, The Bar is mostly small rocks, sand, and grass, not a real breakwater built from locking boulders, and it is quite simple to step out of your boat there and maneuver the craft across to the other side; the interruption can in fact be a welcome chance to get out of the cockpit. (See Fig. 14.) Charles Island and The Bar are parts of Silver Sands State Park, and on the mainland the park includes some of the Silver Beach area, where paddlers may park and launch into The Gulf.

Between The Bar and Milford Harbor's mouth is The Gulf, a pleasant, sheltered, squarish bight between Charles Island and Welches Point southeast of the Milford Harbor entrance, which is in the northeast corner. Once at the harbor entrance, all that is left is to paddle up the narrow but not crowded waterway between the slips, and then take the boat out beside the ramps, which are about 0.7 nmi in from the entrance, on the right near red nun #16.

At low tide, incidentally, approach Milford Harbor's mouth from the south and not the west, as a sandy shoal extends south from Burns Point, the west side of the entrance; squeeze into the harbor with the red nuns to port.

**Fig. 14.** *The Bar and Charles Island, Milford, Connecticut. The launching site at Silver Sands State Park, Milford, looks out across The Gulf.*

## Launching Sites

Note: "CTCAG" after the site name means that a description of the launching site may be found online in the Connecticut Coastal Access Guide. "ConnYak" after the site name means that ConnYak, Connecticut Sea Kayakers, has a brief description of the site on their Web site at www.connyak.org/.

# 2.1   Southport Boatyard (CTCAG)

### Address/Location

Harbor Road, Fairfield, CT; 41°07'46.2"N, 73°17'08.7"W.

### Getting There, Parking, and Fees

Driving either east or west along I-95, take exit 19, for Center Street. From the west, turn right at the first intersection, which is with Center Street. From the east, follow the exit ramp along a curve to the left; it will become first Pease Avenue, then cross US Route 1, then become Jelliff Lane. Center Street intersects after a block and crosses under I-95; turn left and cross under I-95.

Continue along Center Street, cross under the railroad tracks, and at the intersection with Pequot Avenue, cross over while bearing slightly left. Continue to the intersection with Harbor Road and make a sharp right turn, to the southwest. Drive past both Westway Road and Old South Road. The Southport Boatyard will be on the left.

A parking lot is available. No fees are charged.

### Launching

No special considerations are involved.

### On the Water

Even outside the entrance to Southport harbor, waves and tidal currents usually transmit little power. The bottom drops off gradually, and only after one has travelled 0.5 nmi from the harbor's mouth has the water outside the channel reached depths greater than 2 fathoms. If a recreational bay kayaker stays 0.25 mile from shore, there are many easy trips for 4 nmi or more in either direction.

# 2.2 *Brewster Street Boat Launch* (CTCAG)

### Address/Location/Appearance

Brewster Street, Bridgeport, CT; 41°09'10.4"N, 73°13'12.7"W. (See Fig. 15.)

**Fig. 15.** *Brewster Street Boat Launch, Bridgeport, Connecticut*

### Getting There, Parking, and Fees

Coming from the south or west on I-95 North, take Exit 24, but comimg from the north or east on I-95 South, take Exit 25.

From I-95 Exit 24, take the Black Rock Turnpike exit, bear left onto King's Highway, then bear right onto Black Rock Turnpike, which changes its name to Brewster Street when it crosses Caulfield Street.

From I-95 Exit 25, the Fairfield Avenue and Route 130 exit, turn left onto Fairfield Avenue. After 0.45 mile, turn left onto Ellsworth Avenue. If you miss this turn, Brewster Street crosses Fairfield 0.23 mile farther along; turn left onto it.

Follow Brewster Street almost to its end; look for a ramp with walls rising on each side. There is usually parking off-road and along Brewster Street for five cars, but power boaters with trailers park there, too.

No fees are charged.

## Launching

Be aware of the powerboat channel's path as you pull away from the ramp and head south out of narrow Cedar Creek. However, there are no other notable hazards, rocks, or currents.

## On the Water

The view along the west side of Fayerweather Island, as the end of the peninsula forming the east side of Cedar Creek is called, is worth appreciating, especially the sight of the bright white, disused lighthouse beside a grove of trees above marsh grass, all beneath a hot blue sky. Approaching low tide, before the rocks and stones off the island's tip have become exposed, gulls and other seabirds wait placidly in the small salt meadow there for the emergence of the perches on which they will stand to pick their meals out of the catered buffet which they hope the turned, incoming tide will bring to them.

A popular quick trip from this launching site goes out around Penfield Reef and back.

# 2.3   Long Beach (CTCAG)

### Address/Location

Oak Bluff Drive, Stratford, CT; 41°09'26.7"N, 73°08'24.2"W.

### Getting There, Parking, and Fees

Take Exit 30 off I-95. If exiting I-95 North, take the ramp to Sikorsky Airport, then bear right onto Lordship Boulevard (called Hollister north of I-95; also called Route 113 south of I-95). If exiting I-95 North, follow the signs to Sikorsky Airport and proceed along Lordship Boulevard (Route 113).

Drive through Stewart B. McKinney National Wildlife Refuge (Great Meadows Salt Marsh). At end, where Route 113 turns sharply left, turn right onto Oak Bluff Avenue and proceed to the beach at the end of street. Turn right and drive parallel to the beach; both Lewis Gut, on the backside of this barrier beach, and the Sound are accessible from the far end of the parking area.

A parking lot is provided. No fees are charged.

### Launching

If you plan to paddle in Lewis Gut on the back side of Long Beach, consult tide tables; Lewis Gut is shallow, 1 to 2 feet at mean lower low water (MLLW).

### On the Water

Long Beach is an exposed location, but one where the water deepens only gradually: the 1-fathom line lies about 500 yards offshore. Alongshore paddlers can go west for about 1.1 nmi or east about 2.0 nmi; beyond those limits one must deal with Bridgeport Harbor's entrance channel or the Housatonic River, respectively.

Birders may find Lewis Gut attractive, with about 1.5 nmi of channels, many cutting through a tidal marsh.

# 2.4 Point No Point

### Address/Location/Appearance

Washington Parkway and Beach Drive, Stratford, CT; 41°08'54.1"N, 73°07'46.7"W. (See Fig. 16.)

**Fig. 16.** *Point No Point, Stratford, Connecticut. A kayaker prepares to launch from the halfway point in a trip from Brewster Street to Wilcox Park.*

### Getting There, Parking, and Fees

Route 113 throws a loop out around Sikorsky Airport on the peninsula between Bridgeport and the Housatonic River; the west end of the loop is anchored at exit 30 off I-95, and the east end passes under I-95 just east of exit 32.

From the west on I-95, take exit 30 to Route 113 (here, Lordship Boulevard) through undeveloped open land to where it turns sharply to the left (northeast). Go straight on Stratford Road, and then take the fourth street to the right, Washington Parkway, which has a center strip dividing southbound traffic from northbound and lies between 2nd and 1st Avenues. Follow Washington Parkway to the end.

From the east on I-95 South, take exit 32, turn left onto West Broad Street, go east one block, and turn right onto Route 113, going due south as Main Street. After passing Sikorsky Airport, Route 113 turns right (west-northwest). Not straight ahead but at a 45° angle to the right is, again, Stratford Road. Follow Stratford Road to Washington Parkway, which from the east comes after Jefferson Street and then 1st Avenue. Turn left onto Washington Parkway (south) and go to the end.

There is parking available either in a small lot or along Beach Drive. No fees are charged.

### Launching

There is a small, sheltered beach between breakwaters on the shore closest to the restaurant on the west side of Washington Parkway.

### On the Water

Point No Point is either a convenient stopping place or a terminus of bay kayaking trips to or from the west side of Bridgeport or, to the east, The Gulf and Milford.

# 2.5  *Charles E. Wheeler Wildlife Management Area* (CTCAG)

### Address/Location

Court Street, Milford, CT; 41°11'01.0"N, 73°06'05.7"W.

### Getting There, Parking, and Fees

From either west or east, take exit 34 off I-95 and turn right (west) onto Bridgeport Avenue. Drive almost 0.4 mile and turn left (south) onto Naugatuck Avenue. Follow that for almost 0.5 mile and after it bends left turn right onto Milford Point Road. That street bends right, then left, then on the right passes Deerwood Avenue; turn right onto Court Street, the next street, and drive to the end.

There is a small parking lot. No fees are changed.

### Launching

This entire area is shallow at low tide, although not impassable.

### On the Water

All told, there must be several miles of narrow waterways within the Wheeler WMA, and naturalists could hardly ask for better along this coast. To get to the passages behind Neils Island, it may be necessary to paddle north to the Housatonic and then duck into the next opening, about 300 yards downstream.

# 2.6  Silver Sands State Park (CTCAG)

### Address/Location

Silver Sands Parkway/Samuel A. Smith Lane, Milford, CT; 41°12'18.8"N, 73°04'15.2"W. (See Fig. 14 on page 39.)

### Getting There, Parking, and Fees

From either east or west, take exit 35 off I-95. Follow the connector (Schoolhouse Road) southeast to US Route 1 (here, Bridgeport Avenue). Turn left (east) and after about 0.15 mile take the third right onto Silver Sands Parkway. Follow this south across Meadowside Road and into the park. Drive past the main parking lot, turn left at the tee intersection onto the service road, offload at the beach, and return the car to the parking lot.

No fees are charged.

### Launching

This shore is well sheltered and usable at all tides, although a boat may have to be walked out a ways to float.

### On the Water

The Gulf itself is charming, and recreational paddlers can go out to Charles Island, Welches Point, or west toward the Housatonic. There are no known hazards, but stay alert to swimmers and acrobatic (and fast!) parafoil waterskiers in front of the beach.

# 2.7   *Wilcox Park (CTCAG)*

### Address/Location/Appearance

Shipyard Lane, Milford, CT; 41°13'07.9"N, 73°03'19.6"W. (See Fig. 17.)

**Fig. 17.** *Wilcox Park, Milford, Connecticut. The boat ramp is just left of center in this picture, which was taken facing upstream. The gazebo, a landmark for finding the ramp when paddling upriver into Milford Harbor, is to the right.*

### Getting There, Parking, and Fees

Route 162 crosses both creeks, which enlarge to form the two arms of Milford's waterways, Milford Harbor to the west and Gulf Pond to the east. The Milford Harbor crossing is in the center of town, with the town library in its southeast angle. On the library's east side is the entrance to the boatyard and Wilcox Park. Drive in all the way to the end to find the boat ramp and parking spaces.

From east or west, take exit 39 off I-95 and come southwest on US Route 1 (here, Boston Post Road), but only for a short distance; Route 1 veers right, while Cherry Street continues straight. Follow Cherry Street for about 0.7 mile to its intersection with Gulf Street. Turn left onto Gulf Street and go about 0.2 mile to the intersection with Route 162.

Turn right onto Route 162 and go past Harborside Drive on the left to Shipyard Lane just before the library. Turn left and drive all the way in, twists and turns required; look for the gazebo.

### Launching

There are no special considerations here, other than paying attention to slippery surfaces and a narrow waterway busy with powerboat traffic.

### On the Water

Go about 0.8 nmi to the harbor mouth. If the whim strikes, duck under the Gulf Bridge to the east and investigate Gulf Pond; otherwise, paddle out into The Gulf.

The Gulf is a square, 1 nmi on each side, and protected on three sides, open only to the southeast. The corners of the square are the harbor entrance, the base of The Bar, Charles Island, and Welches Point. Maximum low tide depth is about 20 feet on the line between Charles Island and Welches Point.

# 2.8  *Gulf Beach* (CTCAG)

### Address/Location

Gulf Street, Milford, CT; 41°12'40.4"N, 73°02'49.2"W.

### Getting There, Parking, and Fees

Follow directions into Milford as though going to Wilcox Park (which see), but rather than turning off Gulf Street onto Route 162, stay on Gulf Street and drive about 0.85 mile. Go across the Gulf Bridge, which spans the entrance to Gulf Pond, and after about 300 yards look for Gulf Beach on the right.

There are parking spaces. No fees are charged.

### Launching

Put in at a small, sandy beach into a cozy bay; what could be better?

### On the Water

See the remarks for Wilcox Park about The Gulf and Gulf Pond, as well as the chapter narrative. This is a well-sheltered location for a beach, even from the east to southeast. It is open only to the south to south-southwest.

# CHAPTER 3
# New Haven to Old Saybrook

*T*HE CITY OF NEW HAVEN surrounds the largest notch in the Connecticut coastline. That cut marks the outflows of the Quinnipiac and Mill Rivers, although neither stream, in our time, is so forceful that it seems capable of gouging out New Haven's harbor. That capacious, busy harbor is halfway along the northern side of Long Island Sound, equidistant from Throgs Neck, New York and Watch Hill, Rhode Island.

Branford lies adjacent to New Haven—well, East Haven, actually—on its eastern border; after Branford come in order to the east the towns of Guilford, Madison, Clinton, Westbrook, and Old Saybrook.

This chapter describes the opportunities for paddling to be found east of New Haven, or more specifically, east of East Haven, beginning at the town of Branford. Although there are launching sites that face New Haven Harbor (the one at Lighthouse Point Park with kayak rental and instruction being probably the best known), the conditions and risks near the harbor's water are, for this book's taste, too colored by the presence of heavy shipping in an urban setting.

Around the corner from New Haven Harbor, however, is a priceless coast of islands, rocks, and salt marshes cut by gentle tidal rivers: this treasure goes on for about 10 nautical miles (nmi), when it is replaced by arcs of sandy beaches, capped by Hammonasset Beach, which sweeps 2 miles out along the west flank of a narrow peninsula that protrudes well out into the Sound.

After East Haven, the first three towns along this coast—Branford, Guilford, and Madison—have made launching spaces available to

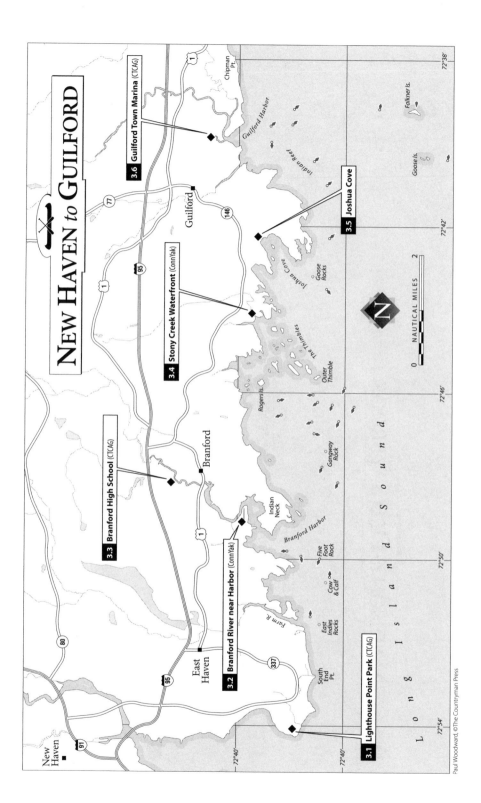

# NEW HAVEN to GUILFORD

**3.6 Guilford Town Marina** (CTCAG)

**3.5 Joshua Cove**

**3.4 Stony Creek Waterfront** (Conn'Yak)

**3.3 Branford High School** (CTCAG)

**3.2 Branford River near Harbor** (Conn'Yak)

**3.1 Lighthouse Point Park** (CTCAG)

New Haven

Guilford

Branford

East Haven

Guilford Harbor

Chipman Pt.

Indian Reef

Falkner Is.

Goose Is.

Joshua Cove

Goose Rocks

The Thimbles

Outer Thimble

Rogers Is.

Gangway Rock

Indian Neck

Branford Harbor

Five Foot Rock

Cow & Calf

East Indies Rocks

Farm R.

South End Pt.

Long Island Sound

N

NAUTICAL MILES

0        1        2

72°38'

72°42'

72°46'

72°50'

72°54'

72°40'

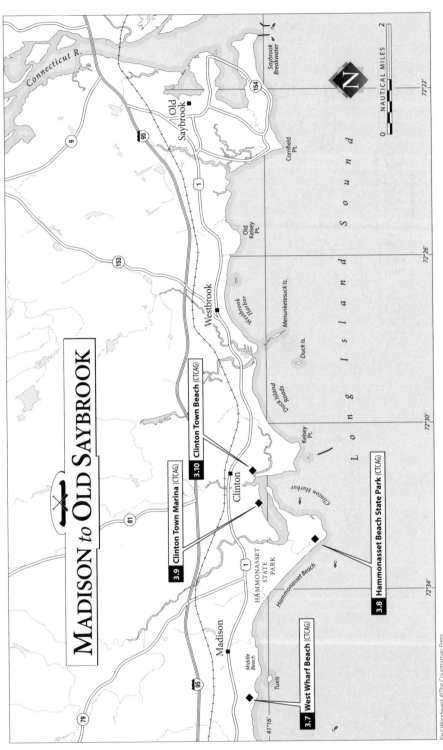

MADISON to OLD SAYBROOK

**3.7** West Wharf Beach (CT CAG)

**3.8** Hammonasset Beach State Park (CT CAG)

**3.9** Clinton Town Marina (CT CAG)

**3.10** Clinton Town Beach (CT CAG)

Madison

Middle Beach

Tuxis

HAMMONASSET STATE PARK

Hammonasset Beach

Clinton

Clinton Harbor

Kelsey Pt.

Westbrook

Westbrook Harbor

Menunketesuck Is.

Duck Is.

Duck Island Roads

Old Kelsey Pt.

Cornfield Pt.

Old Saybrook

Connecticut R.

Saybrook Breakwater

*L o n g    I s l a n d    S o u n d*

79

95

81

1

153

9

95

1

154

41°16'

72°34'

72°30'

72°26'

72°22'

N

0    NAUTICAL MILES    2

Paul Woodward, ©The Countryman Press

cartop boaters, and the state has contributed to paddling with sites in Branford and Guilford; added to these are a few precious locations where access to the Sound is possible and happens not to have been blocked just yet. Some of these facilities collect fees, but others do not. Ten sites in these three towns shall be described, plus a mention of Lighthouse Point Park in East Haven. Get ready for some of the most enjoyable paddling on the Connecticut coast.

The border between East Haven and Branford runs up the middle of a small river called Farm River on the nautical charts and East Haven River on the road maps; whatever its name, there appear to be no public launching sites along it.

There are, however, good launching sites along the Branford River, the next river to the east, which empties into Branford Harbor. If you launch at Branford River and enter Branford Harbor, notice that the channel crosses the harbor by proceeding along 245° magnetic (m) (reciprocal 65°m) until it is close to the west side of the harbor, although the harbor is not particularly shallower in the middle or to the east; nonetheless, boat traffic may be concentrated in the gap less than 0.2 nautical mile (nmi) wide between red nun #4 and Johnson Point, which forms the west side of the harbor's mouth. Once a paddler has rounded Johnson Point closely and gone over toward the Farm River, a little playground 0.5 mile square presents itself: shallows, rocks, two islands, and in the middle of the other shore, Farm River Gut between Horton Point and Kelsey Island, impassable perhaps when the tide is well out.

Paddlers starting from the Branford River have the choice of a launching site behind the high school football field, more than a mile upriver from the state boat launch. This site gives paddlers time to concentrate on the natural sights on the river itself.

Beyond paddling on the Branford River, kayakers leaving the Branford River can exit Branford Harbor along its east side, round Indian Neck, and be 2 nmi from The Thimbles. There are three small islands south to southeast of Indian Neck, from west to east Clam, then Sumac, then Spectacle; tiny Sedge Island is barely a punctuation mark in the gap between Clam and Sumac Islands, an extension of the Squaw Rocks to the northeast.

## From Joshua Cove to The Thimbles in October

The small harbor of Stony Brook directly onshore from The Thimbles is popular with boaters and sightseers, so finding parking within a comfortable kayak-carrying distance of the docks or launching ramp can be a problem, especially on weekends. The map shows other possible starting points somewhat east of the islands, particularly on and around Sachem Head; one is at the end of Trolley Road at the north end of an inlet opening to Long Island Sound to the south and beside the entrance to the waterway into Great Meadow Wildlife Management Area. There are two little beaches to launch from; between them a rock jetty extends west toward a channel leading north up into an expanse of salt marsh enclosed by low wooded slopes on its inland sides.

In the clear cool forenoon of an October day forecast to reach summery temperatures, out on the jetty two young fishermen celebrated catching a silvery fish about 18 inches long; a bluefish, suggested a lady standing nearby. She had come to scout the area before being joined by visiting friends to dig clams in the inlet's flats but had arrived somewhat late and also had not made allowance for the full moon tide, which was pushing wavelets perceptibly higher up the beach as we watched. A man and woman arrived at the beach in a large, outboard-powered skiff and said that the incoming tide had inundated the mudflats off the beach an hour or more since; they lived in a cottage on a small island in the inlet barely a quarter mile toward its mouth from where we stood, and could wade to their house at low tide.

The water in the inlet was as turbid as green pea soup. I expected it to clear as I approached the inlet's mouth, but instead found myself unable during the whole trip to see my white paddle blades through even a foot of water. Beyond the inlet and the first several islands, I pulled in close to the rocks of the next islet, thinking that I might see crabs or minnows, but here too the water was quite opaque and after noting an assortment of four or more species of healthy-looking seaweeds attached to the rocks I turned my attention to the rocks themselves, which were peach-pink granite.

Already the scenery had set me thinking of the Baltic. This little jewelbox of an archipelago appeared to be a version in miniature of the larger one close by the Swedish coast east and southeast of Stockholm. There the redness of the granite bedrock is due to uranium that releases radioactive radon gas, which in that region's weathertight dwellings creates a danger to health and is deemed responsible for a significant portion of the incidence of lung cancers in that region. The granite of The Thimbles is red for the same reason and poses a similar risk.

I worked the kayak around to the south side of the island and, even though forced a half dozen boat lengths from its shore by waves breaking on a field of detached boulders, I couldn't miss a bright mirror flash from halfway up the face of the cliff, about 20 feet high at this point, which came, I saw as the waves washed me in towards the cliff base, from the cleaved surface of a large salmon-flesh feldspar inclusion a good 2 inches square; only part of a considerably larger mass.

Fastened solidly into the rock face to my left—I was now well into the wave surge zone—there was a cleat aligned horizontally about 4 feet above mean high water level, and 5 feet directly above that an eyebolt, also horizontal. I spent several minutes trying to work out how this configuration would be useful and decided that a boat with a bow anchor out to the south, toward the Sound, could get a stern line ashore to this island, fish the line down through the eyebolt, which would serve as a fairlead raising the line above the chafing boulder tops just in front, and down to the cleat. I couldn't imagine anchoring by just tying up to the rock alone, with waves and probably often enough, as now, wind pushing my craft toward these rocks. I backed the boat out of the pocket where it had been rocking in the waves, fending off with light prods of the paddle, so as to be able to see up onto the brow of this island, but saw no person, only two weathered bare wood silver-gray armchairs comfortably side-by-side, looking southward across the Sound. How wonderful, I thought; do they come out here regularly to sit by each other's side to watch the dawn or the sunset, and are they young or old, wealthy or plain, old lovers or new? Was it they or their fathers who put in the cleat and fairlead, and who came to visit them in a boat so big that its draft exceeded

*(continued)*

## From Joshua Cove to The Thimbles in October, *cont.*

the depth of the water off the gentle slopes of the rest of the island's shore, which seemed to offer a much easier access route?

I set off west-southwest toward The Thimbles again, but intentionally looked around to see what birds I could see, and directly to my left, perhaps 50 feet up and 100 feet away, flying toward the islands ahead and overtaking me, was what appeared to be a large gull at first. But after a couple of seconds I saw that it had a tail too long and long wings too broad near their tips to be a gull. It overtook me rapidly and then changed its flight pattern by inserting a brief glide between every fifth to eighth wing flap.

I worked on the idea that it could be a rough-legged hawk, as that buteo is long-winged and long-tailed and habitually intersperses short glides and brief bouts of flapping; this bird didn't fit the rough-legged's profile, though: too early, for one thing, too slender for another, and as it pulled well ahead of me and showed its rear silhouette, during the glide much too much dihedral and in each wing too strong and exaggerated an S-curve. It was not looking for prey or a perch on the islands and ignored the groves atop the nearer Thimbles, but lifted just enough to clear the treetops and continued out of sight. It was a northern harrier, presumably migrating along the coast.

Immediately—and did I hear or imagine a sizzling rush of air past my right ear?—a gray falcon shot past the boat perhaps three paddle lengths away, only several yards above the water; it had no russet anywhere but showed some patterning on the sides of its head. It was smaller and a little slower than a peregrine, and flew in shallow bounds, very much like a pigeon: a merlin. They are said to hunt small birds, including swifts and swallows, by chasing them down from behind in full flight, near-incredible testimony to astonishing reserves of speed and startling aerobatic talents. While the one that passed me was not loafing, he, or more likely she (the females are bigger) was only in a middle gear, with several higher gears to go.

Once I arrived at The Thimbles, I found an enchanting and entertaining miniature playground for anyone in a small boat. Children in canoes could have days of fun chasing each other through the inter-island passages or pouncing upon each other pirate-like out of hiding places behind small headlands. I found myself zigzagging from one island to another, from sunlight to shadow, through a yard-wide cleft spanned by a neat footbridge out to the edge of the island grouping to look back upon it from outside.

About the only thing you cannot do there is land to investigate the islands by foot; signs saying "PRIVATE. KEEP OFF" poke up from piers and the low-lying bedrock shores. Still, nothing prevents you from paddling right along the steep sides of the islands and looking up into the bushes and trees or pulling into seagrass in the lee of an islet for lunch. This day, some bushes had turned vermilion in every leaf, and all the leaves of some trees had turned bright yellow, especially some with soldierly upright silver-gray trunks with vertical striations. Several times small birds flitted between low branches as I came upon them, somewhat like tufted titmice in habit but with pale, sulphur-yellow sides and with backs and wings with a greenish cast; I had no binoculars and could not follow them on foot so had only glimpses, but a small flycatcher did come to mind.

And all day long from island to island, from island to mainland, from mainland to island, coastwise, too, and even heading out across the Sound was a ceaseless traffic of dragonflies and butterflies. For some reason, perhaps because it was an unseasonably warm day and perhaps the last best chance to pick some protected cubbyhole for overwintering, The Thimbles were suffused with lepidopteran dissatisfaction and unrest. Monarchs were moving coastwise, probably in migration, but sulphur and cabbage butterflies were moving locally, and other species, too.

Leaving from and arriving at one island with a beautiful house, beautiful lawns, beautiful trees, and beautiful flower gardens were what when I was young I called "Graptas" after my grandfather's instructions, but which now are named polygonias or anglewings; they are butterflies that like fruit trees and that used to be easier to spot back when there were still meadows and pastures in southern New England with old apple and pear trees watching over buttercups and lady's tresses. To a quick glance they appear brown and ragged, but watched closely at leisure their tattered plainness unfolds into

*(continued)*

---

**From Joshua Cove to The Thimbles in October,** *cont.*

exquisite gradations of orange through umber on the upper surface and microscopically detailed patterns etched onto the lower. Our local species overwinter as adults, and some are found in the maritime provinces of Canada southward, which makes it seem very likely that these individuals were polygonia seeking shelter out in The Thimbles.

Another type of butterfly that I saw several times this day is not so easily explained, to date. These had perhaps a 1.75-inch wingspan with wings bright orange-red above, bordered with black and with a regular, rounded outline, looking so much like a butterfly a child might draw with colored markers that I thought a careful pass through the butterfly guide must reveal it to be some species I'd presumably not noticed before between the skippers, the admirals, and the fritillaries. However, I have not been able to find any mention of such a butterfly, and I wonder whether it could have been a local form of a usual species, or an exotic that has found a niche as the native species have succumbed, or a completely new species previously unnoticed and at home perhaps only in the equally unusual environment produced by The Thimbles.

As I paddled out around the headland of the outermost island of the group, I experienced the feeling of moving beyond the shelter of land, but here, as elsewhere in The Thimbles, in miniature. The nature of the change at this boundary was mostly visual; the calm out on the Sound had no deeper oceanic notes, and crossing the line between inshore and offshore waters was not accompanied by any consciousness of added risk: all this day I paddled carelessly upon an inland sea.

---

Red flasher #28 lies about 0.8 nmi practically due south (182°m) from Spectacle Island and makes a reasonable southern boundary for recreational paddlers; just beyond, the bottom drops off to more than 40 feet, and larger and considerably faster traffic up and down the Sound may pass by.

Red flasher #26 lies 1.4 nmi away on a course of 116°m (reciprocal 296°m) from #28 and is on the southern edge of a cluster of reefs much beloved by fishermen. Again, this marks a reasonable southern limit for recreational paddlers. This same flasher is 2.1 nmi from and almost due south of 196°m (reciprocal 16°m) the flagpole at the head of the little channel into Pine Orchard; the house chimney on Outer Thimble Island is 1.5 nmi from that same flagpole, on 172°m (reciprocal 352°m), and on many days the waters between Outer Thimble and the coast are a paradise for paddlers, who may if they wish play hide-and-seek throughout an archipelago of sweet islets, whether well tended or left to be themselves.

We have introduced The Thimbles as though a paddler had launched from Branford Harbor, but almost all the kayaks among The Thimbles will have set out from Stony Creek, the nearest mainland, where parking may be difficult to come by in summer and even in the fall; therefore, it is useful to think of The Thimbles as a destination that may be approached laterally, so to speak, from the west from Branford, but also from the east.

The Thimbles themselves are in Branford, but the town boundary with Guilford, the township to the east, runs north between Bear Island and Hoadley Neck and then onshore up the little creek at the west side of the base of Hoadley Neck, so launching from Guilford still puts a paddler in the water close to The Thimbles. A little over 1 nmi east of Headley Point, past Harrison Point and Leetes Island, is a beach beside the watercourse leading into the Great Pasture Wildlife Management Area. This beach is beside a small parking lot at the end of Trolley Road, which goes west off Old Sachem Head Road, and is at the northeast end of squarish Joshua Cove, which lies along the west side of Sachem Head and which contains Foskett Island and Horse Island.

The town of Guilford has more launching sites, too, located east of Sachem Head. Two that charge no fees are the Guilford Town Marina at the end of Old Whitfield Street on the point of land facing south between Sluice Creek and the East River, and the East River State Boat Launch on Grass Island, which geographically is in Guilford but which you reach by driving through Madison. Both these sites place a paddler at the northern end of Guilford Harbor with a narrow, buoy-marked channel through the shallows. Once a kayaker has come south to the level of Guilford Point on the western side of the opening into the harbor proper, the bottom falls away enough to permit paddling, say, southwest to Mulberry Point even at low tide. The town marina is described below, but the East River site has been omitted as redundant; see the online Connecticut Coastal Access Guide (www.lisrc.uconn.edu/coastalaccess/) for more information.

From the marina ramp to green nun #11 beside Guilford Point is 0.35 nmi, and from there to Mulberry Point is 0.8 nmi; this leg is crossed by the traffic lane leading into the West River, so find the buoy pairs green can #3/red nun #4 and green can #5/red nun #6 southeast and northwest, respectively about 0.3 nmi from Guilford Point, and take precautions.

Paddlers also should be aware that a busy east-west traffic lane passes barely 0.25 nmi south of the end of Sachem Head. Its margin is marked by red nuns #16, #20, and #22, going from east to west. Red nun #16 is 0.9 nmi from Mulberry Point, bearing 214°m, and all three are in very nearly a straight line 1.8 nmi long oriented east-west (103°m; reciprocal 283°m). We mention this because the proximity of the channel to the shore corresponds to a bottom that comes up from about 40 feet to less than 20 in under 150 yards: be alert for patches of stronger current, upwellings, and accentuated waves near the reefs and rocks off Sachem Head, as well as powerboat traffic relatively close to shore.

From red nun #20, the middle marker in the line of three and the one directly south of Sachem Head, over to The Thimbles in 2 nmi. Thus, from the Guilford Marina ramp to The Thimbles is about 4.4 nmi. Paddling out and back, with lunch and exploring in the middle, would make a pleasantly vigorous day outing for paddlers with boats that cruise at 3 knots or better.

East of Guilford Harbor, the coastline and the offshore features simplify, and rather than reefs and islets close in there are sandy beaches that form shallow arcs. The easternmost stretch of beach, southward-facing Hammonasset Beach, barely curves at all, and the 3-fathom line comes in quite close to shore. So, in 6 nmi or so the feel of

Connecticut's Long Island Sound shoreline changes completely, from sheltered archipelago to exposed surf zone. True sea kayaks would be most at home off these beaches, and kayakers in these waters should be justly confident in their abilities to assist themselves and others in case of overturning; although, to be sure, that should be true of paddlers anywhere.

Along this stretch of beaches, paddlers may launch from at least four of Madison's beaches, including magnificent Hammonasset; all charge parking fees, but on the positive side, all have space to accommodate a group outing. These launch sites are: West Wharf Beach, Surf Club Beach, East Wharf Beach, and Hammonasset Beach State Park. However, Surf Club Beach and East Wharf Beach are not described here, because West Wharf Beach has facilities enough to make those two other nearby sites redundant.

Let us consider next the coastline east of Hammonasset Point. If you have ridden the New York-to-Boston train along the Connecticut coast, you may have noticed an area where there are several views of narrow waterways and clean marshes; the creeks and coves may have held anchored rowboats, and great blue herons may have risen from the salt meadows, which seem secluded and quiet—except for the racket of the train. This rural-appearing area that takes one back in time to early years along a tidal river centers on Westbrook, extending into Clinton to the west and Old Saybrook to the east.

Not visible from the train, the shoreline of these towns has had four scoops taken out, first starting from the west by Clinton Harbor, then Duck Island Roads, then Westbrook Harbor, and finally either the eastern lobe of Westbrook Harbor or an unnamed embayment into which feed Cold Spring Brook, the Oyster River, the Back River, and the outflow of the wetlands behind Plum Park Beach, north-northwest from Cornfield Point.

East from Cornfield Point, the shoreline of Old Saybrook undulates to the east past Guardhouse Point, reaching Lynde Point at the western side of the mouth of the Connecticut River. There are cartop boat launching sites in Old Saybrook between 1 and 2 nmi upstream along the river's western bank, in North Cove in particular, but we shall leave paddling on that river to those with better knowledge of local conditions, having watched powerboats bash their way through standing waves and be jostled by the strong swirling current.

Hammonasset Point juts out into Long Island Sound 7 nmi west of Cornfield Point; it is the southernmost tip of the peninsula called Willard Island. Tucked up in the angle between the "island" and the east-west shoreline, to the northeast, is Clinton Harbor. Paddlers may launch from Hammonasset Beach State Park, near the point, and come around Willard Island and then along the side of the 0.8-nmi-long spit of land that extends to the northeast, ending in Cedar Island. Beyond that slender promontory, only a 0.3-nmi-wide passage is left into the back side of Clinton Harbor and between it and the mainland the band of water is only 0.25 nmi wide. The entire harbor is shallow, and the channel in this sharply bent passage is narrow and changeable, altering its course from time to time.

The waterfront is bounded by the Hammonasset River on the west and the Indian River on the east, and across from Cedar Island the Hammock River drains the extensive marshes behind Hammock and Kelsey Points on the east side of the harbor. Among them, the Hammonasset, Indian, and Hammock Rivers have more than 2 nmi accessible to paddled boats at the proper tide.

Those who wish to experience tidal waters sheltered to an unusual degree could hardly do better than to try Clinton Harbor. There is a launch site along the 1.1-nmi-long Clinton waterfront at the town marina.

East of Clinton Harbor, a breakwater 0.6 nmi long extends south-southeast from Stone Island, which lies about 0.23 nmi off the squarish neck of land whose southern corners are Hammock Point and Kelsey Point. This structure, called the Kelsey Breakwater, ends 0.4 nmi shy of red nun #8, which marks the Sound's east-west traffic lane along the northern shore. Paddlers who wish to pass between Clinton Harbor and Duck Island Roads to the east have to choose, of course, whether to go north or south around this barrier. The marine chart sees fit to note that tide rips occur between the breakwater and red nun #8. The same chart shows a narrow natural channel between the breakwater's north end and the shore (closer to the latter); as this channel is not shown to have been dredged by humans, it must be scoured by a current. Therefore, locally strong currents, perhaps with turbulence, may be encountered at either end of the breakwater; we would, however, opt for the north end.

A paddler who wanted to go from Hammonasset Point to Kelsey Point directly, crossing the mouth of Clinton Harbor, could do so in a single leg, which left the breakwater to the south by paddling 1.75 nmi heading 88°m (reciprocal 268°m).

East of Kelsey Point, a paddler is in Duck Island Roads, with a choice of things to see. The Clinton-Westbrook town line comes down to the water 1.25 nmi along the shore from Kelsey Point, and Westbrook is home to those inviting marshes seen from the window of the train. These marshes are fed and drained by the Menunketesuck and Patchogue Rivers; both meet just before the shore and share a single outlet to the Sound at the eastern extreme of Duck Island Roads. Reach this opening by paddling 78°m (reciprocal 258°m) for 1.75 nmi from Kelsey Point. This entrance, by the way, is reminiscent of the one into Milford Harbor, as it too has a narrow, straight channel marked by buoys and shoal water to each side. The Patchogue River, the eastern stream, has a dredged channel; the Menunketesuck is less engineered and more bucolic. Try these rivers between half and high tide.

Westbrook Harbor is east of Duck Island Roads. Between the two lies slender Menunketesuck Island, essentially the exposed north-south humpback of an otherwise submerged peninsula; paddling between the island and the shore to take a shortcut into the harbor would be best attempted with the tide more than halfway in: the water is very shallow north of the island.

Sea kayakers intent on seeing Connecticut's coast by traveling from point to point may instead strike out from the southern end of Menunketesuck Island to Cornfield Point, 3.35 nmi away on a heading of 106°m (reciprocal 286°m).

The mouth of the complex of streams that issues from the land north of Cornfield Point is not quite so far away, 3 nmi, heading 86°m (reciprocal 166°m); these small rivers, the Oyster and the Back, would best be approached at half to high tide.

Here we have reached Old Saybrook, having crossed from Westbrook about 0.9 nmi west of the Oyster and Back Rivers' common mouth, and have paddled about 6.5 nmi from the launch site in Clinton Harbor. Clearly, launch sites choser to Old Saybrook would be welcome. Luckily, although shore access is not plentiful along this shoreline, there is one site in Westbrook: Kirtland Landing on the Menunketesuck River.

We have strong reservations about paddling closer to the western side of the mouth of the Connecticut River than, say, Cornfield Point, at least without close examination of the weather and tide conditions right on the spot.

Although there is no city at the mouth of the Connecticut River, the river is navigable by commercial shipping for 45 miles upstream to Hartford. One could take the position that canoeing or kayaking along this stretch would be like pedaling a bicycle in the breakdown lane of an interstate highway.

Furthermore, near the entrance to the river, which concerns us here, the interaction between the tidal currents and waves of Long Island Sound and the river's outflow can set up conditions dangerous to small craft in general. Here is what the National Oceanic and Atmospheric Administration's (NOAA) *United States Coast Pilot* (Volume 2, Chapter 8: "Eastern Long Island Sound") has to say: "Currents: At the entrance the currents have considerable velocity at times and always require careful attention, as the tidal current of the Sound often sets directly across the direction of the current setting out or in between the jetties. This condition is reported to be especially dangerous during the first 3 hours of ebb tide."

And:

"Because of river discharge, the ebb current usually will be considerably stronger than the flood."

Paddlers might also want to be aware that at least one series of tidal current charts for Long Island Sound (the Model-Predicted Tidal Current Charts generated at the University of Rhode Island with the support of NOAA's Office of Sea Grant) shows both ebb and flood currents to be stronger at the mouth of the Connecticut River than in front of the mainland to either side, and these currents to have peak speeds two-thirds of those at The Race at the western end of Fishers Island, which is the measuring stick for current speeds throughout the Sound: hardly anyplace in Long Island Sound has tidal currents faster than The Race, certainly no place described in this book.

## Launching Sites

Note: "CTCAG" after the site's name means that the online Connecticut Coastal Access Guide contains a description of this site. "ConnYak" after the name means that ConnYak, Connecticut Sea Kayakers, describes this launching site on their Web site.

# 3.1   *Lighthouse Point Park* (CTCAG)

### Address/Location

Lighthouse Road, East Haven, CT; 41°14'35.8"N, 72°53'39.4"W.

### Getting There, Parking, and Fees

Drive south on Route 337 (here, Townsend Avenue), turn right onto Lighthouse Road, enter Lighthouse Point Park, and drive on Park Avenue to Lighthouse Point. From Lighthouse Point, follow the road southeast until it reaches Morris Creek and turns back northeast.

To get to Route 337 from the west driving along I-95 North, take exit 50 to Lighthouse Point; drive along Woodward Avenue to Main Street, and turn right onto Route 337.

From the east, take exit 51 from I-95 South onto Frontage Road; after about 0.8 mile, turn left onto Route 337. Go south past the Tweed–New Haven Airport; the Lighthouse Road intersection is about 2.3 miles south of I-95.

Parking lots are more than ample. Fees are charged.

### Launching

Cartop boat launching facilities are available beside Morris Creek, not at the ramp for trailered boats, which faces west into the entrance to New Haven Harbor.

### On the Water

Cross in front of the mouth of Morris Creek and then Shell Beach to reach Morgan Point. West Silver Sands Beach will appear, and east of that South End Point. After 1 nmi comes the mouth of the East Haven River (also shown as the Farm River) and a squarish cove, about 0.5 mile on each side. From the launch site to the river's mouth is 2 nmi. From the river to Stony Creek, onshore from The Thimbles, is 5 nmi. From the river's mouth to Branford's Town Marina is about 2.7 nmi, not allowing for skirting around areas of powerboat traffic.

# 3.2   *Branford River near Harbor (ConnYak)*

### Address/Location

Goodsell Point Road, Branford, CT; 41°15'57.5"N, 72°49'00"W.

### Getting There, Parking, and Fees

From east or west on I-95, take exit 54 for Branford and drive south on Route 740 (here, Brushy Plain Road) to US Route 1. One may cross Route 1 and continue toward town; Bushy Plain Road has become Cedar Street. Cedar Street bends slightly to the right where Harrison Street forks off to the left and ends at South Main Street, which is Route 794; turn right. Pass Rogers Street on the left and turn left on the next crossing street, Monroe Street. Monroe Street crosses Elm Street and changes its name to Kirkham Street; it goes over the railroad tracks, skirts an open area beside the river, and bends right, heading west. Immediately after this bend, it is crossed by Harbor Street; turn left on Harbor, heading south. Pass Driscoll Road, cross over a brook, and then turn left onto Goodsell Point Road. The launch site is 200 yards along on the left.

Alternatively, turn right on Route 1, then after about 0.9 mile, turn left (south) onto Route 142. Continue south for 0.5 mile, then turn left onto Stannard Avenue. This road reaches Harbor Street after about 0.7 mile; go straight (Stannard becomes Goodsell Point Road); the launch site is 200 yards ahead on the left.

Parking is available at the site. No fees are charged.

### Launching

No special launching considerations are known.

### On the Water

Paddlers can travel more than 2 nmi upstream between grassy riverbanks, for despite Branford being as densely settled as it is, the housing tracts have somehow failed to encroach closely upon the river. There is a launch site at the high school on the left bank (going upstream) and some distance of river to enjoy above that before the diminishing stream goes under I-95.

Downstream, the river opens out into Branford Harbor and the Sound. Bend to the right around the point, staying alert for boats entering and leaving the very densely occupied wharves on the outside of the bend and then on the south side of the point. The best practice might be to hug the point until you can paddle due south across the channel into the unfrequented shallows, then continue toward the river's mouth along the south side of the channel.

# 3.3  *Branford High School (CTCAG)*

### Address/Location

East Main Street, Branford, CT; 41°16'46.2"N, 72°48'20.6"W.

### Getting There, Parking, and Fees

East Main Street is US Route 1 in Branford where it lies just south of I-95. Branford High School is situated on the south side of Route 1, midway between exits 54 and 55 from I-95. Coming west on I-95 South, use exit 55 and drive west on Route 1 approximately 1 mile; the high school will be on your left. Driving east on I-95 North, take exit 54 and turn right onto Bushy Plain Road to head south to Route 1; turn left onto Route 1. The high school will be about a mile along on the right.

Drive in behind the school. The launch site is between the football field and the river.

There is ample parking. No fees are charged.

### Launching

No particular concerns are known.

### On the Water

This site sits midway along a 4-nmi stretch of quiet river, thus offering paddlers hours of travel through easy, sheltered surroundings. Those wishing to venture out to the Sound could also start from here; read the comments about the Branford River mouth site above.

# 3.4 Stony Creek Waterfront (ConnYak)

### Address/Location

Thimbles Island Road, Stony Creek, CT; 41°15'58.8"N, 72°45'22.7"W.

### Getting There, Parking, and Fees

Leetes Island Road comes south from exit 56 on I-95 and crosses Route 146, and there (or shortly after) it becomes Thimbles Island Road. Follow it into Stony Creek, but stop before arriving at the area with wharves; there is a small sandy beach on the right for launching, and if there are any parking spaces to be found, they will most likely be at this end of the street.

Parking beside the street is permitted (watch for exceptions), but unoccupied spaces may be scarce. No fees are charged.

### Launching

There are no special concerns.

### On the Water

A marked north-south channel runs down the middle of the inlet the launch site faces. As there may be as many kayaks on the water around Stony Creek as in all the rest of Long Island Sound on a summer weekend, powerboats maneuver tentatively but should be granted unobstructed passage in their channel. See this chapter's narrative for observations on traffic beyond Outer Thimble.

# 3.5  Joshua Cove

### Address/Location

Trolley Road, Branford, CT; 41°15'37.0"N, 72°42'42.5"W.

### Getting There, Parking, and Fees

If coming along I-95, get off at exit 58 and drive south on Route 77 toward Guilford. Cross Route 1 and continue to Route 146 and turn right (west). Drive 0.9 mile and watch for Sam Hill Road entering from the right at an abrupt blind left turn, a passageway beneath the railway, and then a small street, Sachem Head Road, straight ahead where Route 146 turns abruptly right. If coming east on Route 146, the turn onto Sachem Head Road requires turning through 120° or so, a very sharp turn in a place with blocked lines of sight.

Drive 0.5 mile along Sachem Head Road and bear right onto Colonial Road at a fork. About 300 yards on, take another right fork onto Old Sachem Head Road. After 0.2 mile, turn right onto Trolley Road; the street sign may be missing. Drive to the small narrow parking lot at end. Try to park so as not to obstruct vehicles that may arrive later.

There is parking for four to six cars. No fees are charged.

### Launching

Launch either from the beach to the Sound side or from the path on the marsh side of the old raised roadbed. However, note that the tidal current through the gap in the old causeway can be swift and turbulent.

### On the Water

The salt marsh to the north is the Great Harbor Wildlife Management Area; the navigable waterway up into the marsh peters out beyond the wooded knoll in the marsh, though.

To the south, Joshua Cove holds Horse and Foskett Islands, both of which have their charms, especially the latter. The Thimbles are 2 nmi to the west. To the east, around Sachem Neck, are Guilford Harbor and several small rivers. Be aware that an east-west channel along the Sound passes close by Sachem Head. See chapter narrative for remarks on alongshore piloting here.

# 3.6 Guilford Town Marina (CTCAG)

### Address/Location

Old Whitfield Road, Guilford, CT: 41°16'20.7"N, 72°39'58.8"W.

### Getting There, Parking, and Fees

This site is easy to find. Use exit 58 off I-95 and come south on Route 77 toward Guilford and simply continue straight across Route 1 and then Route 146. The road changes its name to Old Whitfield Street. Go past the fork where New Whitfield Street bears right; take the smaller street that continues straight after a slight jog to the left. Drive all the way to the end.

A parking lot is provided. No fees are required.

### Launching

No special considerations are needed.

### On the Water

This site is sheltered from winds except out of the southeast; if heading out onto the Sound, get information on conditions you may encounter once beyond the harbor's protection.

Birders should find this site a remarkable starting point, because there are miles of small rivers (the West, East, and Neck) whose mouths are all within 0.5 mile of this marina; all three flow through tidal marshes and salt meadows, promising many pleasant prospects.

# 3.7   *West Wharf Beach* (CTCAG)

### Address/Location

West Wharf Road, Madison, CT; 41°16'16.1"N, 72°36'17.0"W.

### Getting There, Parking, and Fees

West Wharf Beach is the middle one of three beaches in Madison along the east-west shoreline of the large embayment between Sachem Neck to the west and Hammonasset in the east. The other two, Surf Club Beach to the west and East Wharf Beach, are described in the Connecticut Coastal Access Guide; their positions may be useful to know if a kayaker needs to head toward a takeout location in an emergency: Surf Club Beach, 41°16'25.2"N, 72°35'38.9"W, and East Wharf Beach, 41°16'21.6"N, 72°35'21.6"W. For launching along this shore, however, West Wharf Beach may suffice.

The beach is located at the end of West Wharf Road, which runs south from US Route 1 west of downtown Madison, east of where Mungertown Road connects Route 1 to I-95 at exit 60 and west of where Route 79 does likewise at exit 61. The West Wharf Road turnoff is about 0.35 mile west of the Route 79 and Route 1 intersection, but about 1.7 miles from Mungertown Road; therefore, if driving along I-95, it will almost always be quicker to take exit 61.

There is ample parking at this town beach. Fees are charged.

### Launching

The fishing pier should provide shelter when launching, but be prepared for Sound conditions once out of its shadow, for this is an exposed stretch of the coast.

### On the Water

From the east-southeast to the west-southwest, the closest land is about 3 nmi away; due south is Long Island, somewhere between Jacob's Point and Mattituck Inlet, 17 nmi away. If you look very carefully out along 135°m (give or take a few degrees), between Hammonasset Point, Plum Island, Montauk Point, and Block Island, you may catch a glimpse of Senegal.

# 3.8  *Hammonasset Beach State Park (CTCAG)*

### Address/Location/Appearance

Boston Post Road (US Route 1), Madison, CT; 41°15; 48.4"N, 72°21'14.7"W. (See Fig. 18.)

**Fig. 18.** *Hammonasset Beach State Park, Madison, Connecticut. The cartop boat launching site in the state park is almost at the end of the point, beside a jetty. The parking lot is a short walk back along the roadway to the left.*

### Getting There, Parking, and Fees

If driving along I-95, take exit 62 and follow the Hammonasset Connector (itself a divided highway) south to Route 1 and then across that into the park. Once in the park and having paid any entrance fee, drive all the way out to the point; take the second exit from the traffic circle in the park, not the first, which leads to a beach but not one with a cartop boat launching site.

Parking spaces are located a couple of hundred feet from the launching beach beside a jetty; a paved lane connects the two, so you may drive close to the beach, offload, and then return your vehicle to the parking area.

Fees are charged according to the Connecticut State Park schedule.

### Launching

You will be launching from a promontory that juts a mile out into the open Sound. Red nun #10 is 0.43 nmi from the launching beach, bearing 252°m, and the NOAA chart shows tide rips between the jetty and the buoy. There are rocks offshore and a submerged boulder near the buoy, plus a submerged boulder just inshore of the buoy. Consider launching from the beach on the north (landward) side of the jetty if you plan to paddle in front of Hammonasset Beach. If your destination is Clinton Harbor or Duck Island Roads, choose the south side.

### On the Water

West Wharf Beach is 3 nmi away on a heading of 309°m (reciprocal 129°m) from the north angle of the jetty. Hammonasset Beach itself is 1.5 nmi long. One good thing about the location is that regardless of the visibility, if you head northeast you will surely hit land. On the other hand, if a southwest wind has built up strong surf, you will have to land despite it.

# 3.9 *Clinton Town Marina (CTCAG)*

### Address/Location

Riverside Drive, Clinton, CT; 41°16'08"N, 72°31'51"W.

### Getting There, Parking, and Fees

Take exit 63 from I-95 and drive south on High Street (Route 81) to the end. There, turn right onto Central Avenue, go about 100 yards, and turn left onto Hull Street. Hull Street meets US Route 1; turn right onto Route 1, drive about 0.25 mile, and turn left (south) onto Grove Street. Drive on Grove Street past Pratt Road and then Laffingwell Road (Neck Road, on the other side), then West Grove Street (Shell Road); turn right onto Riverside Drive. The town marina is about 200 yards along on the left.

A parking lot is available. The Town of Clinton charges a fee.

### Launching

No special considerations are known.

### On the Water

The deeper part of the Hammonasset River channel begins in front of the marina, so this site should be usable at all tides. Upriver, the channel is narrow and unmarked, while the remainder of the river is shallow.

# 3.10 Clinton Town Beach (CTCAG)

### Address/Location

Waterside Lane, Clinton, CT: 41°16'08.7"N, 72°31'13.4"W.

### Getting There, Parking, and Fees

Waterside Lane, which ends at the Clinton town beach, comes south from US Route 1 (here, East Main Street) 0.3 mile west of where Route 1 and Route 145 meet and 0.35 mile east of the Route 1–Route 81 intersection. Therefore, if driving west on I-95 South, one might choose to avoid downtown Clinton by taking exit 64, turning left onto Route 145, and driving south on it to a T-intersection, turning right to stay on Route 145, and continuing for about 1.7 miles to Route 1. Turn right onto Route 1, go 0.3 mile, and turn left onto Waterside Lane.

From the west (or as an alternate route from the east), if driving on I-95 North, take exit 63, come south on Route 81, and do the little dance described for the Clinton Town Marina to get to Route 1: Route 81 (High Street), right onto Central Avenue, left onto Hull Street, and thence to Route 1. However, turn left onto Route 1, then drive about 0.35 mile and turn right onto Waterside Lane.

The Clinton Town Beach has a parking lot. Fees are charged.

### Launching

The water off the beach is shallow, and the west side of the channel is 150 yards from shore. The Hammock River, which flows north along the back (east) side of the beach, is actually deeper than the water in front of the beach, and this depth carries around the north end of the point of land on which the beach sits and then into the main channel.

### On the Water

With three small tidal rivers, Clinton Harbor, and—around to the east past Hammock and Kelsey Points—Duck Island Roads and then Westbrook Harbor to investigate, recreational paddlers should find a route for every mood, tide, and weather condition.

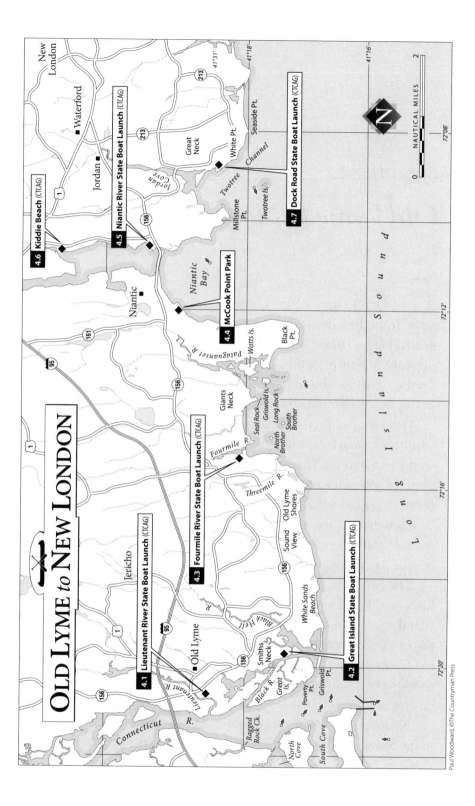

# OLD LYME to NEW LONDON

**4.1** Lieutenant River State Boat Launch (CTCAG)

**4.2** Great Island State Boat Launch (CTCAG)

**4.3** Fourmile River State Boat Launch (CTCAG)

**4.4** McCook Point Park

**4.5** Niantic River State Boat Launch (CTCAG)

**4.6** Kiddie Beach (CTCAG)

**4.7** Dock Road State Boat Launch (CTCAG)

New London

Waterford

Jordan

Great Neck

White Pt.

Seaside Pt.

Jordan Cove

Twotree Channel

Twotree Is.

Millstone Pt.

Niantic

Niantic Bay

Patagansett R.

Watts Is.

Black Pt.

Giants Neck

Seal Rock

Griswold's Is.

Long Rock

North Brother

South Brother

Fourmile R.

Threemile R.

Old Lyme Shores

Sound View

White Sands Beach

Black Hall R.

Old Lyme

Jericho

Lieutenant R.

Smiths Neck

Great Is.

Poverty Pt.

Griswold Pt.

Black R.

Ragged Rock Ck.

Connecticut R.

North Cove

South Cove

L o n g   I s l a n d   S o u n d

N

NAUTICAL MILES

0                    2

41°31'

41°18'

41°16'

72°20'

72°16'

72°12'

72°08'

Connecticut

Paul Woodward, ©The Countryman Press

# CHAPTER 4
# Old Lyme to New London

*F*ROM OLD LYME TO NEW LONDON, or in terms of coastal geography from the Connecticut River to the Thames River, is about 12 nautical miles (nmi); along I-95, one may drive from riverbank to riverbank in little more than 15 minutes. Nevertheless, although this is a rather short section of the Connecticut coastline, it is very much worthy of consideration by paddlers.

However, paddlers are unlikely to explore this stretch unless they start from a launch site somewhere along it, for the Connecticut River on the west and the Thames River on the east partition it effectively from the rest of the coast, at least as far as recreational kayakers and canoeists are concerned.

Fortunately, there are several public launching sites, two along the east side of the Connecticut River, one halfway between that river and Niantic Bay, and another midway between Niantic and New London.

The two sites along the Connecticut River are the Lieutenant River State Boat Launch, which is for cartop boats only, and the Great Island State Boat Launch. Strictly speaking, neither of these sites places a paddler in the main waters of the Connecticut River, much less in Long Island Sound, but because there are few better places for watching birds and appreciating the native marsh life of the Sound's ecosystem from a boat, they are included here.

Before going out onto the Connecticut River itself and from there to the Sound, local information, updated to the very hour, should be obtained. Paddlers should note that, almost uniquely along this section of the Connecticut coastline, a great circle line-of-sight out between 110° magnetic (m) and 130°m fails to encounter land much this side of the Canary Islands and Morocco!

It may also be true that the shoal water off Griswold Point at the eastern side of the river's mouth exists because the river's sediment burden is deposited so rapidly that it is able to balance the increased current—river and tidal combined—that the decreased water depth provokes. One cannot always equate shallow water with a languid current.

Paddlers starting from the Great Island launch site, however, may explore on their own or choose to follow one of the routes mapped and posted on the information board. There must be approximately 5 nmi of waterways available to paddlers behind Great Island, if one includes the Black Hall River and its tributaries. This is a true natural treasure of the coast to be savored repeatedly.

The Lieutenant River launch site, north of Great Island, provides access to a small tidal river with about 2.5 nmi of stream navigable by paddlers. It opens onto the Connecticut River about 0.5 nmi downstream, and in either direction travels through low pastures and marshland. Because the launch site is limited to cartop boats and parking is limited to six cars, the burden that recreational activity places upon the river is slight, as it should be with kayaks and canoes.

East of Great Island, the next chance to paddle on the Sound comes at the Four Mile River State Boat Launch; it too is in Old Lyme, but East Lyme is right across the river. This site, like Great Island, has much more mud than water at low tide; it may be difficult to put in, paddle, or take out at much below half tide. Once in the water, though, a quick push past the railroad bridge 0.2 nmi downstream brings a paddler into the northwest corner of a trapezoidal rabbet cut into the East Lyme shoreline. To the east, for 0.5 nmi—about half the width of this small bay—Rocky Neck State Park abuts the water. Over in the northeast corner are Watts Island and the mouth of the Pattagansett River, and out in the bight are North Brother, South Brother, and Griswold Islands, plus a host of rocks and ledges, particularly in the easternmost third. Pleasure boats abound, but because of the broken, rocky bottom they will typically be proceeding gingerly, and this area, although densely built up with cottages east of the park and out along Black Point, offers much to see.

Leaving this bight by the southwest, around Hacketts Point, as though one were going back to the Connecticut River, a sea kayaker will find 3 nmi of beaches before Griswold Point at the river's mouth, with its potential complications. Leaving to the southeast, along the west side of Black Point, and turning east, a paddler opens Niantic Bay.

Millstone Point on the east side of the bay's mouth is 2.1 nmi distant on a heading of 74°m (reciprocal 254°m). The head of the bay will remain farther away than its sides throughout the crossing, so at the midpoint of this leg, the closest shore is about 1.1 nmi ahead or behind. The lane for powerboat traffic occupies most of the width of the bay: green can #7 floats beside Threefoot Rock 0.35 nmi offshore from Attawan Beach, and red nun #8 is beside Black Rock, itself 0.3 nmi west of Bay Point; 0.85 nmi separates these markers.

Since so much of the mouth of the bay is navigable, the paths of powerboats entering or exiting the bay tend to fan out, crossing the line from Black Point to the red flasher and bell #6, which is 0.45 nmi southwest of Millstone Point; they are usually traveling rapidly and up on their step by then and may have trouble seeing a kayak—and indeed may not be expecting a low, slow, fragile craft to be out there at all. Everything that could be done to increase the chances of your boat being seen would be worthwhile if you were to take this route.

A paddler might be prudent to come north into Niantic Bay and cross where it is narrower. For example, from green can #7 to red nun #8 is 0.8 nmi on a heading of 90°m (reciprocal 270°m).

Another tactic would be to take advantage of the fact that a dredged channel extends 0.3 nmi southwest from the exceptionally narrow cut in The Bar, the roadbed that forms the head of Niantic Bay and separates it from the Niantic River. This entrance channel's beginning is marked by green #1, which is just under 0.7 nmi from green can #9, itself 0.55 nmi north of green can #7 and about 0.1 nmi (220 yards) south of Wigwam Rocks. There should be no traffic on your landward side before the channel and no traffic trying to cross your path; cross the channel and the same should apply on the other side.

Onshore (northwest) from green can #9 is the McCook Point Town Beach, where cartop boat launching is allowed, and a parking lot is provided. Both a fee and a permit from the town are required, but on balance this may be the best launching or takeout site within Niantic Bay.

North of The Bar, there are two launching sites onto the Niantic River: the big Niantic River State Boat Launch close to the channel out to Niantic Bay; and Kiddie Beach, 1.5 nmi upstream, fronting Keeny Cove. The Niantic River forms in effect a boat basin 3 nmi long, in heavy use, sheltered from the Sound but accessible only through a dredged channel barely 40 yards wide at best between concrete walls and riprap. It is a sluiceway swept by a fierce tidal current. When a large powerboat goes through the channel beneath the highway bridge, bucking the tide, it is hard to see where a kayak or canoe would go to hide: powerboats 30 feet long and more rightly consider this passageway their access to the Sound, but a paddler ought not to. Thus, these two launching sites should be used only to try the Niantic River, not Niantic Bay.

The environment east of Niantic consists of a nuclear power plant, beaches, reefs, and boulders, all facing Twotree Island Channel, which is 0.2 nmi wide and in places more than 60 feet deep as it squeezes between the steep shore and Bartlett Reef (and the eponymous Twotree Island). NOAA's *U.S. Coast Pilot* speaks of Twotree Island Channel being used by "light tows" when there is "an adverse current in the Sound," as "tidal curents turn about 1 hour earlier along the north shore than in the middle of the Sound." It also mentions flood currents with a speed of 1.2 knots and ebb currents of 1.6 knots; it advises strangers (speaking of powerboats and sailboats) to use it with caution. The same could probably be said for paddlers.

To spice the environment even more, some concern has been expressed about lapses in perimeter security about the Millstone nuclear plant; just in case of overly enthusiastic attempts to defend the plant, kayakers might want to simply avoid Millstone Point altogether.

On the eastern shore of the small bight east of Millstone Point is the Dock Road–Pleasure Beach State Boat Launch. Given the concern about security at the power plant, it is convenient that this launching site is presently unusable for launching trailered boats. A bar separates the water off Pleasure Beach from Jordan Cove to the north; the entrance is about 0.5 nmi to the northwest. The 3-fathom line swings into this bight and is barely 300 yards from the launching ramp; Africa is somewhere off in the east-southeast; Twotree Island Channel has a strong current and boat traffic. Even so, a sea kayak in capable hands can venture along such shores by staying within, say, 50 yards of land, and a succession of points and beaches may be visited in this manner, wrapping around the headland of Great Neck to the southeast, then east, then northeast up toward New London Harbor.

The progression of features around Great Neck goes: White Point, Megonk Point, Seaside Point, the entrance to Goshen Cove, Goshen Point itself, then Ocean Beach, Osprey Beach, and the lighthouse (flashing a red light at 89 feet in elevation every six seconds) marking the entrance to New London's harbor.

The interactions between the Thames River and the Sound begin before the beacon, and Goshen Point or Ocean Beach might be as far around Great Neck as a paddler would want to go: in any event, the scenery becomes distinctly urban beyond there. Rather than try to identify each beach or point of land, consider turning around when your alongshore course consistently swings north of 75°m; that should still provide 5 nmi of paddling out and back from Pleasure Beach.

Route 156, also known as Shore Road in Old Lyme, follows the Eight Mile River south from East Haddam, finds the Connecticut River, passes through Old Lyme crossing I-95 and the Lieutenant River, then goes through Black Hall and South Lyme, all the while bending eastward and remaining a mile or less from the shoreline, to arrive in Niantic. There it crosses The Bar and angles northeast into Waterford and past then as far as New Haven, but even there on Great Neck it is the baseline, the road from which all the launching sites in this chapter may be reached.

I-95 is useful for moving parallel to Route 156 at high speed, but if you have no particular need to drive along I-95, you will be able to arrive at any of these launching sites by following Route 156 to their respective turnoffs. Exit 70 off I-95 will put you on Route 156 alongside the Connecticut River; exit 72 closest to Four Mile River; exits 72, 73, or 74 will bring you into Niantic; exit 81 (note: no exits numbered 77, 78, or 79) brings you closest to Pleasure Beach.

*The cove at the east side of the mouth of the Thames River, around Avery Point. Beyond the point of land ahead lies a swift-flowing, urban river, but this cove and the waters to the south and east offer pleasant paddling.*

## Launching Sites

Note: "CTCAG" after the site name means that a description of the launching site may be found online in the Connecticut Coastal Access Guide. "ConnYak" after the site name means that ConnYak, Connecticut Sea Kayakers, has a brief description of the site on their Web site at www.connyak.org/.

# 4.1  *Lieutenant River State Boat Launch (CTCAG)*

### *Address/Location*

Shore Road (Route 156), Old Lyme, Connecticut; 41°18'50.9"N, 72°20'14.3"W.

### *Getting There, Parking, and Fees*

The launch site is in the northwest angle of the bridge that carries Route 156 over the Lieutenant River.

If you are coming from the west along I-95 North, get off at exit 70 and turn right onto Route 156; the Lieutenant River bridge is 0.4 mile farther on, and the launch site will be on the near bank, on the right-hand side of the street. If, however, you are coming along I-95 South from the east, exit 70 from that direction lets you off east, not west, of the Lieutenant River. Turn left onto Lyme Street, drive 0.75 mile, turn right onto Ferry Road, drive 0.3 mile, turn right onto Route 156, and cross the river. The launch site is on the left.

There is parking for several vehicles, and no fees are charged.

### *Launching*

There are no special considerations about this popular site beside a tidal river.

*On the Water*

The Lieutenant River joins the Connecticut about 0.6 mile down-stream; the bottom drops off rather abruptly along this riverbank to 3 fathoms or more. Remember that the first three hours of ebb are reported to be the time of the strongest current.

Upstream, expect more than 2 nmi of relaxed paddling in a setting that retains much rural character and native wildlife.

# 4.2   Great Island State Boat Launch (CTCAG)

### Address/Location/Appearance

End of Smith's Neck Road, Old Lyme, Connecticut; 41°17.27'N, 72°19.50'W. (See Fig. 19.)

**Fig. 19.** *The Great Island State Boat Launch at the end of Smith's Neck Road, Old Lyme, Connecticut.*

### Getting There, Parking, and Fees

Get on Route 156 coming south beside the Connecticut River. Coming from the east, you can also drive west along Route 156, although you'll be out of sight of the Sound. I-95's exit 70 (see Lieutenant River launch site directions) or exits 71 or 72 may be convenient. If using exit 71, come south on Four Mile River Road 0.7 mile to its end at Route 156; if using exit 72, come south on Routh 449, a divided highway connector that ends at Route 156 after 0.5 mile: in both cases turn right (west).

Coming south on Route 156, drive just over 1 mile past the Lieutenant River and turn right onto Smith Neck Road; bear left at the fork in the road, and go to the end.

Coming west along Route 156, cross the Black Hall River and turn left onto Smith Neck Road after just over 0.5 mile.

There is a surfaced parking lot sufficient for a dozen cars or more. Fees are charged, at least in season.

## Launching

Launch and recover more than two hours to either side of low tide.

## On the Water

As the *Connecticut Coastal Access Guide* says, "This is a wonderful coastal location." There are four principal areas to explore: (1) to the right, bearing right at the fork to enter a long backwater, (2) upstream again, but bearing left to follow the Back River that joins the Connecticut River, (3) to the left and continuing straight into the large salt pond shielded from the Sound by Griswold Point, and (4) to the left, but wrapping around Smith's Neck to head up the Black Hall River, which enters the northeast corner of the salt pond east of Smith's Neck. Try them all. This is an exceptional bit of geography for New England—unpolluted, unexploited, and for the most part uninhabited; a remnant of the region's heritage.

# 4.3   Four Mile River State Boat Launch (CTCAG)

### Address/Location/Appearance

Beyond the end of Oakridge Drive, Old Lyme, Connecticut; The mouth of Four Mile River is at 41°17.96'N, 72°14.92'W. The ramp is at 41°18.49'N, 72°15.16'W. (See Fig. 20.)

**Fig. 20.** *Four Mile River State Boat Launch, Old Lyme, Connecticut. Long Island Sound is beyond the railroad bridge downstream of the launching site, but launching should be attempted only when the tide is at least partway in.*

### Getting There, Parking, and Fees

Get onto Route 156 halfway between Old Lyme and Niantic. If coming along I-95, follow instructions for exits 71 and 72 for the Great Island launch site. If driving east along Route 156, pass Old Lyme Shores, the railroad tracks, and Point O' Woods. Turn right onto

Oakridge Drive. If you see Four Mile River Road or Route 449 on your left, or Rocky Neck State Park on your right, you have gone too far.

If driving west along Route 156, pass Rocky Neck State Park, the Route 449 connector, and Four Mile River Road. Pass Mill Creek Road on the right and 0.4 mile farther on turn left on Oakridge Drive.

Oakridge Drive enters the Ridgewood neighborhood. There will be a fair-sized parking lot at the end of the tarred road, and a smaller road out of the lot on the far side down to the boat launch. Deer and other animals frequently cross the small twisty road down to the launch, and if you approach quietly you may see herons feeding.

There are no fees. There is space for several cars close to the water, although much of this area might be required by maneuvering vehicles with trailers, and for dozens of vehicles in the upper lot.

## Launching

This site is usable above half tide.

## On the Water

The river upstream of the launch is navigable for about 1 nmi, but it is the Sound that beckons kayakers. See the main description in this chapter.

# 4.4 McCook Point Park

### Address/Location

Atlantic Street, Niantic, Connecticut; 41°19'04.6"N, 72°12'01.5"W.

### Getting There, Parking, and Fees

A few hundred yards west of Route 156's intersection with Route 161, which comes south from exit 74 off I-95, a street runs south from Route 156; there are signs near the corner reading "McCook Park" and "St. Agnes Church." Pass the church to your left, cross the railroad tracks, and follow the street around a sweeping arc to the right. Turn left onto Atlantic Street, which bends right. Partway through the bend and on your left is the park entrance.

Cartop boat launching is by permission granted by the Town of Niantic. Apply at the Department of Recreation office. Rates are: day pass, $5 residents, $15 nonresidents; season pass: $25 residents, $75 nonresidents.

### Launching

Launching is from a sandy beach well away from boat traffic and currents.

### On the Water

Head south to round Black Point, cross the bight beyond, and enter Four Mile River to arrive at the state launch site: about 3.5 nmi. Attempting to enter the Niantic River is not recommended.

Beware of fast boat traffic fanning out from the end of the entrance channel south of the east end of The Bar, or coming into Niantic Bay heading for the channel.

# 4.5  Niantic River State Boat Launch (CTCAG)

### Address/Location/Appearance

Second Street, Niantic, Connecticut; 41°19.60'N, 72°10.53'W. (See Fig. 21.)

**Fig. 21.** *Niantic River State Boat Launch, Niantic, Connecticut.*

### Getting There, Parking, and Fees

From either west or east on I-95, take exit 74 (note: no exits numbered 75 through 79) and come south on Route 161 all the way to its intersection with Route 156 at the water. Turn left, cross The Bar, and turn left onto West Street. Turn left onto Niantic River Road. Turn right onto River Street. Turn right onto Second Street.

Parking is plentiful. Fees are charged. However, cartop boaters may be able to find parking outside of the state lot.

### Launching

The ramps, which face north up the Niantic River, are broad and gently inclined. Better than the ramps is the 100-foot-long beach beside them, perfect for paddlecraft.

### On the Water

Head north. It is needlessly dangerous to try to use the narrow, busy, hard-sided channel to reach the Sound from here.

The Niantic River is more like a working boat basin at its southern end, but it quiets down in the northern part. Paddlers can go about 2.5 nmi north from the launching ramp on quiet water.

# 4.6  *Kiddie Beach* (CTCAG)

### Address/Location

234 Niantic River Road, Waterford, Connecticut; 41°21'09"N, 72°10'36"W.

### Getting There, Parking, and Fees

From Route 156, turn north at intersection with Niantic River Road about 0.1 mile east of bridge at The Bar. Drive north 1.4 miles. Kiddie Beach is on the left.

From I-95 North, take exit 75. Turn right onto Route 1 (Boston Post Road). Drive 1.5 miles; turn right onto Niantic River Road.

From I-95 South, take exit 81. Turn left onto Parkway North. Turn left onto Cross Road. Turn right onto Route 1 (Boston Post Road). After 0.6 mile, turn left onto Niantic River Road.

No fees are charged, but there are only a few parking spaces.

### Launching

Launch from the small beach beside the picnic area into the shallow end of a blind inlet.

### On the Water

Same as for Niantic River State Boat Launch: enjoy the river, but do not attempt to reach the Sound.

# 4.7 Dock Road State Boat Launch (CTCAG)

### Address/Location

Dock Road/Pleasure Beach, Waterford, CT; 41°18'31.9"N, 72°08'53.8"W.

### Getting There, Parking, and Fees

*The Connecticut Coastal Access Guide* has instructions for using exit 82 if coming on I-95 from the east and using exit 72 if coming from the west, but it may be just as convenient, although not optimal in terms of distance, to follow the directions for the Niantic River Boat Launch, that is, to use exit 74 to get onto Route 156 heading east.

After crossing The Bar, drive almost 2 miles to Waterford; turn right onto Route 213. After about 1.5 miles, turn right onto Goshen Road and go to the end; the road changes its name to Dock Road.

### Launching

This launch site is closed to trailered boats at the time of this writing, but cartop boats may still be launched.

### On the Water

Going west to Millstone Point is not recommended. North into Jordan Cove or alongshore to the east to Goshen Point are possibilities for half-day trips from this site.

# CHAPTER 5

# Groton, Stonington, and Westerly

*E*AST OF THE THAMES RIVER, the Connecticut coast blossoms into a paddler's garden of delights. These waters are flushed twice daily by contributions from the ocean brought in by the tides, so they are often clear as greenish glass, and although Block Island Sound and the Atlantic send in their long waves, still, Fishers Island blocks—or at least attenuates—their power. Monotony could never cloud a kayaker's day here, unless one were to tire of views of inlets and islets that change almost by the minute.

For a bayworthy craft, this area presents just enough technical demands to help a paddler continually improve, but there are, it must be realized, places within reach of a morning's paddle where Long Island Sound may test the judgment and ability of even the very best, for less than 5 nmi south of the mouth of the Thames River, off the western tip of Fishers Island, the bottom falls away to depths greater than 300 feet, and the speeds encountered in tide rips may exceed those attainable by any kayak but a sprinting racer: Race Rock has earned its name.

Of the passages between Fishers Island and the Rhode Island shore at Napatree Point and Watch Hill Point, 2 nmi to the former and 3 nmi to the latter, the *U.S. Coast Pilot* is moved to mention "buoys towed under" and "extreme caution."

Along the Connecticut mainland shore, however, conditions are

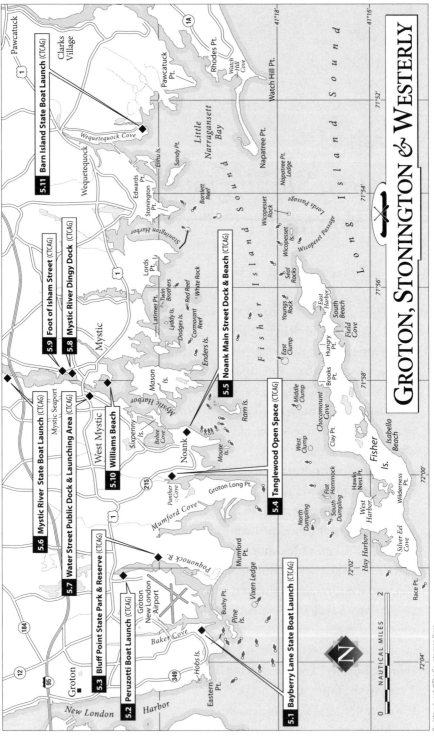

# GROTON, STONINGTON & WESTERLY

**5.11** Barn Island State Boat Launch (CTCAG)

**5.9** Foot of Isham Street (CTCAG)

**5.8** Mystic River Dingy Dock (CTCAG)

**5.5** Noank Main Street Dock & Beach (CTCAG)

**5.6** Mystic River State Boat Launch (CTCAG)

**5.7** Water Street Public Dock & Launching Area (CTCAG)

**5.10** Williams Beach

**5.4** Tanglewood Open Space (CTCAG)

**5.3** Bluff Point State Park & Reserve (CTCAG)

**5.2** Peruzotti Boat Launch (CTCAG)

**5.1** Bayberry Lane State Boat Launch (CTCAG)

NAUTICAL MILES

N

Paul Woodward, ©The Countryman Press

more moderate, and paddlers may expect to encounter demands upon their skill during an average outing no greater than an increased tidal current over shoal ground, perhaps rising above 3 knots, or swirls and upwellings caused by broken rocky bottom just off points of land that protrude into the tidal flow.

This region begins in the west at the mouth of the Thames River and stretches 10 nmi east to the mouth of the Pawcatuck River within Little Narragansett Bay. Most of it, in fact, is called Fishers Island Sound, although we treat it here as though it were part of western Long Island Sound. Indeed, the area is covered in Chapter 7, "Block Island Sound" in the *U.S. Coast Pilot,* under the heading "Fishers Island Sound," not in Chapter 8, which covers western Long Island Sound. In this distance, about nine prominent points of land jut south into the Sound, call it Long Island Sound or Fishers Island Sound: (1) Avery Point, (2) Mumford Point, (3) Groton Long Point, (4) Morgan Point, (5) Mason Point (the tip of Mason Island), (6) the compound Dodges Island, Andrews Island, and Latimer Point, (7) Wamphassuc Point, (8) Stonington Point, and (9) Sandy Point (offshore of Edwards Point). East of these is the roughly northwest-southeast corrugated shoreline of Little Narragansett Bay, whose southern end is closed off by Napatree Beach and Point.

Between these points are coves and rivers: the Poquonnock River, hardly a major stream, emerges between Avery Point and Mumford Point, and the Mystic River, with its more significant flow, cuts its channel mostly west of Mason Island, but in the other gaps between the points are coves, some used as harbors—as in the case of Stonington Harbor between Wamphassuc Point and Stonington Point. Some are narrow, but most more than 1 nmi long. Most of the area within these coves lies shoreward of the 1-fathom line; most of Little Narragansett Bay, in fact, except near the outflow of the Pawcatuck, does so too. Such topography is ideal for recreational paddling, and a paddler who went along the shoreline, in and out of the coves and harbors and also around the islands, would cover more than 40 nmi, at a guess.

A distinctive feature of Fishers Island Sound, however—which paddlers along this shore should bear in mind—is the boating and light shipping channel that runs along its midline, on average about 105° magnetic (m) (reciprocal 285°m). The shipping channel's depths make its usage possible, and the tidal currents keep its waters clear.

From Groton almost all the way to Stonington, Fishers Island stretches out in the south along the near horizon and seems not at all far off: the southern side of Ram Island is a mere 1.6 nmi from Brooks Point on Fishers Island. Yet paddlers should not cross to Fishers Island on a lark, just because it is there; it is recommended that a nautical chart be consulted to see how the crossing might best be accomplished. The author has not paddled out to Fishers Island, but people who have been there as part of a group speak of being swept backwards by the tide, unable to round a point; they seem to have been speaking of experiences in the neighborhood of East Point, beside the Wicopesset Passage, where such currents regularly occur. From examining the National Oceanic and Atmospheric Administration (NOAA) chart (reproduced by Richardson), reading the *U.S. Coast Pilot,* and extrapolating from personal observations off Ram Island and elsewhere along this length of coast, the most sensible route to Fishers Island could be to go to the rock off the midpoint of the south end of Ram Island, paddle 0.50 nmi heading 170°m (reciprocal 350°m) to red flasher-and-bell #20 at the edge of the channel, look both ways, and cross to Middle Clump, marked by green can #21, 0.62 nmi distant, bearing 213°m (reciprocal 033°m). A spine of shoal bearing 152°m (reciprocal 332°m) connects Middle Clump to Brooks Point 0.67 nmi away; it is interrupted, however, by a right-of-way for local traffic marked by red nun #2W 0.20 nmi offshore and green can #1W close in. However, one would be wise to ask for local knowledge first, as well as to make the crossing in a highly visible group of boats.

There are enough launching sites open to the public along the shore between the Thames and the Pawcatuck to enable paddlers to explore this entire region in easy day trips, putting in and taking out at one site.

Groton extends from the east bank of the Thames River to the west bank of the Mystic River; in this span *The Connecticut Coastal Access Guide* lists seven suitable launching sites.

Stonington extends from the east bank of the Mystic River to the west bank of the Pawcatuck, which divides Connecticut from Rhode Island. *The Connecticut Coastal Access Guide* lists four suitable launching sites here, and Williams Beach may also be used.

The Ken Streeter State Boat Launch in Groton on the east bank of the Thames beneath I-95 does not seem inviting to kayakers, because the Thames flows swift and turbulent past the ramp, which faces an urban harbor. Fishing boats with big dual outboards go crashing away upstream, and there seems little sense in pitching a paddled boat in after them, not when the Bayberry Lane State Boat Launch beckons from downstream and to the left around Avery Point.

From Bayberry Lane State Boat Launch, paddlers can range into the mouth of the Thames, up the Poquonnock River, out around Bluff and Mumford Points, and up Mumford Cove with ease, and even the Mystic waterfront lies only 6 nmi away, if one is not distracted by side excursions.

One might launch from Bayberry Lane and proceed south past boats moored in the narrow harborway, then turn west when the opening behind Pine Island south of Avery Point appears. Round Avery Point and come up into the river, into a little recess south of Eastern Point, in front of Shennecossett Beach.

Swing out to Black Rock and from there come southeast (140°m; reciprocal 320°m) along the edge of the Pine Island Channel; 0.65 nmi on this heading brings you to red bell-and-flasher #2 off the west end of Pine Island. Watch for traffic using the channel between Avery Point and Pine Island, too. This can be a busy corner.

With an eye out for traffic, one might go across the channel over to Franks Ledge and Black Ledge. From Eastern Point or Black Rock, go south across Pine Island Channel to the red-green buoy at Franks Ledge (about 0.47 nmi, bearing 194°m, reciprocal 014°m, from Eastern Point) and from there over to Black Ledge to the southeast.

Pine Island is small but attractive, with two main indentations along its southern margin fringed by shell-covered beaches with brows of wild roses. (See Fig. 22.)

Coming around Pine Island, it is possible to cut between it and its

***Fig. 22.*** *The south side of Pine Island, off Avery Point, Groton, Connecticut. This jewel adorns the entrance to the Thames River.*

close neighbor, Bushy Point, which is actually an island, for its connection to Bushy Island Beach is covered by water. At low tide, a kayaker will likely have to get out and pull the boat across the shoal between Bushy Point and the beach to reach the Poquonnock River or the entrance to the passage back up to the Bayberry Lane launching site or to venture up the length of Baker Cove. All these places are better visited some hours away from low tide.

Back at the middle of the southern side of Pine Island, if you wish to paddle across the embayment in front of Bushy Point Beach across to Bluff Point and Mumford Point, there are no particular concerns, other than not to wander so far south that you arrive out in the channel. Vixen Ledge, with red nun #28VL, is 0.53 nmi from the middle of Pine Island, bearing 138°m, and defines the channel's northern edge in this area. Farther east, just east of Mumford Point, its edge is marked by red nun #26, which is 1.46 nmi from Pine Island, bearing 120°m; from Vixen Ledge and #28VL, #26 is 1.05 nmi away, bearing 106°m. Mumford Point itself is 1.2 nmi from Pine Island's central bump, bearing 106°m. This means that a paddler has a lune-shaped area in which to play, with soundings of 25 feet halfway across, and if headings are kept north of 120°m when coming from Pine Island, your boat should not be in the channel.

The peninsula that ends in Bluff and Mumford Points is itself a worthwhile destination. Its 800 or so acres have been designated the Bluff Point Coastal Reserve and have been allowed to remain wooded and undeveloped. A little swimming beach lies along its west side north of Bluff Point, and all around the peninsula are places to pull out kayaks and canoes for resting, picnicking, and enjoying the view. From the top of the bluff the view is even better.

*The peninsula with Bluff Point State Park seen from the water southwest of Groton Long Point. Bluff and Mumford Points offer sandy shores where paddlers can beach their boats and rest. There is also a network of trails through the woods on top of the bluff and a launching site upriver on the west side of the point.*

Paddlers desiring a sheltered tidal river can choose two launching sites on the Poquonnock River; both are practically next to the railroad bridge that crosses the river 1.3 nmi upstream from Bushy Point Beach, which stretches across its line of flow and what would otherwise be its mouth.

## West and East from Noank

Where to go? Which way to turn? My new long white boat was a paddle's length away from the Noank Town Dock and I was still fastening my sprayskirt, while a strong flood current and the Mystic River's outflow along the channel that runs beside the shore were already bearing me off to the southwest. (See Fig. 23.)

**Fig. 23.** *Noank Main Street Dock, Noank, Connecticut.*

Had the afternoon been bright and clear, the points and islands might have stood out from each other and from the background of the mainland and long Fishers Island, which stretched along the southern skyline. However, dull overcast flattened distance, and more than several hundred yards away—say 0.25 mile—not much detail remained within the land's low profiles. I snapped a page from a book of waterproof nautical charts beneath the cords across the foredeck between the cockpit and the heading compass, but eyes that had decided to require new prescriptions for reading and for distance failed to show more than a blurry image of the chart's 10-by-7 nautical miles, when I would have been best served by a blow-up of a circle with a 1.5-mile radius centered on my position. A bearing compass, the excellent, rubber-covered French hockey puck, hung around my neck, but what use was that when I had no way to winkle out the correspondence between the real world and the chart?

*(continued)*

## West and East from Noank, *cont.*

But there lay Ram Island, looking close at hand against the backdrop of Fishers Island at an indeterminate remove behind, and so it was decided to paddle to a destination that the captain of the boat could at least see.

The long white boat with twin brants in marquetry upon the foredeck slipped across the water like a purposeful being, "a bird on the wing," undeflected from its heading.

The buoy just off the near end of the island went by to starboard—the boat was holding close to 4 knots—and a house and trees stood in silhouette against the sunlit southwestern sky, so I took a picture and continued on. The water beneath the boat was transparent, and the rocks and plants upon the bottom, always fascinating, showed up colorful and crisp.

*An islet south of the Noank Town Dock, with Groton Long Point and Bluff Point in the distance. These rocky islets, including Ram Island, are smaller and fewer that in the Thimbles and the Norwalk Islands, but the water quality is in general superior and the paddling can be extraordinarily pleasant.*

I went south around the far end of the island and saw and felt the mystery and force of Fishers Island Sound itself, felt reluctance rise at the prospect of paddling across, a reticence that I could not explain—

*(continued)*

**West and East from Noank,** *cont.*

for the reason, whatever it was, was not distance. It is farther from Sandy Point in Warwick, Rhode Island on Narragansett Bay over to Patience and Prudence Islands, and I have made that trip often without a further thought, except about the screeching cigarette boat that someone flings past Warwick Neck at more than 60 knots, blind with speed. No; it was not the distance, but some energy contained within the waves, some curling at their crests, some unexpected tumbling against the breeze, something that said to ask around before stepping the short way across that strip of water. So I curved the boat around to the west side of Ram Island and into the shadow of the flood current cast by the island.

About halfway along the island, I began to turn left away from its shore, still in shoal water; soon the boat was buffeted by the current sweeping around the island's north end. Without the current, the eelgrass growing up from the bottom not 6 feet below would have stood straight up, but the upper sheet of water slid past at better than 3 knots, bending the top halves of the grass leaves over at right angles and flattening them into a rippling green carpet. I paddled backwards to hold my place above the grass, and let this clear, swift water on Ram Island Shoal flow by. Large jellyfish swept past, distinct and still, as though encased in glass. They were the size of cabbages, and beneath a colorless half-dome they wore bunched petticoats of pastel plum maroon; out to a foot beyond those frilly skirts splayed fat translucent tentacles charged with toxins, enough perhaps to stun a hand-sized fish.

It would be quite easy to become confused among the islands along this part of the Connecticut shoreline; little islets that are barely detectable on a chart seem to be major features of the scenery when seen from certain locations. Paddle a little farther, though, and brand-new points or islands dominate the view.

Northwest of me, a cove that had been hidden when I started out now showed its deep calm harbor sheltering a dozen open boats, hulls white against the dark water. Its eastern side is Morgan Point, its western side Groton Long Point. The bottleneck opening of Palmer Cove is its northwest corner, there is a small pocket in the center of its

*(continued)*

## West and East from Noank, *cont.*

far end, and its northeast corner stretches up as the short sleeve of West Cove. Overhead, flat clouds formed an opaque leaden ceiling, and light came in under them only from the west-southwest. I slid the long white boat into the small bay, then canted it onto its starboard chine so that it curved to port and came alongside Groton Long Point.

Off the point, a man fished from his boat out by a buoy, yellow sky behind him. A fast current swept my boat past boulders close in to the point, and the boat's hull, being narrow, felt as though it teetered on a log and fidgeted more than could be explained by the slightly choppy waves. This "tippy water" is a familiar motif close in to the points in Fishers Island Sound, something separate from either waves or tidal velocities alone. Perhaps obstructions on the bottom—boulders and sharp ridges—heave up vortices that are tilted toward the horizontal by the current to toy with a kayak's hull. On a related note, at any tide there are rocks just barely submerged close to almost all

*Off Groton Long Point, looking west down the length of the Sound, with buoy and fisherman looking like an updated Winslow Homer painting. The alongshore current is stronger than might be expected, and rocks appear from nowhere like humpback whales.*

*(continued)*

## West and East from Noank, *cont.*

these points; they reveal themselves by the circular boils they cause that distort the pattern of the waves.

*Groton Long Point in silhouette beneath rain clouds.*

Groton Long Point has its own barrier reef, concave to the southwest and an echo of Bushy Point Beach, which so improbably blocks off the mouth of the Poquonnock River. The shore from Avery Point to Groton Long Point is open to the southwest and somewhat north of that direction, and the fetch across which waves could build before arriving here equals the entire length of Long Island Sound, something in the neighborhood of 80 nmi on a bearing of 255°m to 260°m (reciprocal 75°m to 80°m). It is not uncommon to find that the wind blows from that direction.

It may be relevant and interesting to read about a short-lived near-squall out of just this direction that I encountered once in front of the arc of Bushy Point Beach. A late afternoon's light breeze strengthened remarkably as the sun neared the horizon, and the waves in the bight between Bushy Island and Bluff Point tripled in height and very nearly had their crests blown off, an indication that the wind was approaching gale force. This alliance of strong wind and energetic waves went on for a busy 20 minutes and then died away as twilight fell. I switched my strobe light on and headed back to Bayberry Lane, well

## West and East from Noank, *cont.*

chastened. How often this occurs I cannot say, but a plausible mechanism can be constructed for an evening squall directed west to east, from light to dark, from warm to cool in autumn, down the long axis of Long Island Sound, and an almost daily squall directed exactly into this pocket, added to the winter westerlies, could help explain the presence of Bushy Point Beach and the Groton Long Point reef.

*Another lovely rocky point of land near Noank, this one to the east, around Mason Island.*

Another trip I remember began from the Noank Town Dock and went east around the south end of Mason Island, on the way to Wamphassuc Point. "Tippy water" again played with the long white boat and made me feel that it was skidding sideways on ball bearings. Past Mason Point, the trip was all that an alongshore paddler might require. There were bits of interesting architecture on the shore, short causeways, a chapel unexplained, a patch where currents flowed in the opposite direction from what I had expected, a bridge, small connected islands, and, around Lyddy Island, where the bottom is called "foul" on a mariner's chart, orange, red, and yellow gardens on the rocks beneath the hull. Rock Island, out by red nun #2R, the favored local roost for cormorants, emitted an acrid plume downwind.

After leaving Mumford Point, turn north into Mumford Cove for more than 1 nmi of paddling beside a quiet shore to the west and the neighborhoods on Groton Long Point to the east. This inlet zigzags between spurs that protrude from one side then the other, and local small boat activity goes on.

A round trip starting from Bayberry Lane and going around Avery Point to Eastern Point, to red flasher #2 off Pine Island, back up and down Baker Cove, up and down the Poquonnock, over to Bluff Point, up and down Mumford Cove, and back to the start covers about 12 nmi, which is a comfortable yet vigorous day's outing in a fast boat—and a considerable amount of exploration compressed into a small area.

No public launching sites are known in Mumford Cove west of Mumford Point.

However, one cove to the east, on the other side of Groton Long Point and in the Tanglewood neighborhood along the east side of Palmer Cove, there is a convenient kayak launching site on Seneca Drive; Palmer Cove is shallow at low tide, so this site may be best suited for use an hour or more from low tide.

The Noank Town Dock has no such limitations, as it borders a channel. From this site, Groton Long Point to the west, Wamphassuc Point and Stonington Harbor to the east, and much of the Mystic River all the way north to Old Mystic are each about 3 nmi away. Middle Clump off Fishers Island is 3 nmi to the south, but that excursion warrants special planning and considerations. All in all, the Noank Town Dock is benignly situated in a most convenient and central location. It is suitable for only light use, though: there is parking for no more than two or three cars.

Northeast of Mason Island over on the mainland there is another excellent access point into Fishers Island Sound and the Mystic River: Williams Beach. Paddling west will bring you to the narrow mouth of the Mystic River; paddling south takes you under the little Mason Island bridge and then out among Andrews, Dodges, and Enders Islands.

**Fig. 24.** *Looking east from Dodges Island toward Wamphassuc Point.*

East of Dodges Island is an embayment about 1.5 nmi wide, bordered on the east by Wamphassuc Point. (See Fig. 24.)

From the southern tip of Enders Island to the tip of Wamphassuc Point is 1.91 nmi on a heading of 92°m (reciprocal 272°m). To make the direct traverse point-to-point even more convenient, buoys serve as wayposts from Enders Island to a little more than halfway across towards Wamphassuc. From the tip of Enders Island to red nun #6 is 0.27 nmi, 74°m (reciprocal 254°m); from #6 to red nun #4 on the south side of Cormorant Reef is 0.25 nmi, 89°m (reciprocal 269°m); from #4 to red nun #2 south of Red Reef is 0.59 nmi, 97°m (reciprocal 277°m). From #2 the tip of Wamphassuc Point is 0.86 nmi on a heading of 94°m (reciprocal 274°m). A long breakwater begins about 150 yards offshore of the point and extends southeast for 0.35 nmi, so if you were to miss the gap between point and breakwater by being too far south, you could be forced into an exposed patch of water through which much of the traffic in and out of busy Stonington Harbor passes. For this reason, a paddler will probably aim for the west side of Wamphassuc Point and work down to its tip by following the shore.

That western shore of Wamphassuc, as it happens, is unusual in having three other points—short parallel prongs—jutting from it, spaced out at almost equal distances (0.2 to 0.25 nmi), and this varied, sheltered topography makes this shore particularly enjoyable for paddlers. About a 0.25 mile farther west than the first of the prongs is the entrance to Quiambog Cove, which even at low tide should be navigable to paddlers for its length of 0.9 nmi. The Washington-to-Boston train blasts through the marsh and across the cove on its low bridge with little or no warning, and close up it seems very loud.

Once at Wamphassuc Point, the issue becomes how to cross the active boating area of Stonington Harbor and reach the west side of Stonington Point, or vice versa. One approach is to avoid the problem altogether and work around the harbor's perimeter, making way as required for boats entering or leaving their slips. The main axis of the harbor is about 0.85 nmi long, measuring from a line connecting Wamphassuc and Stonington Points, and there are two arms that spread out north of the railroad bridge, so a complete exploration of the shoreline could go on for 3.2 to 3.6 nmi. This would make a pleasant afternoon excursion by itself.

A 0.35-nmi-long breakwater was built 0.5 mile south of Stonington Point to cast a wave shadow across the mouth of the harbor, which otherwise would look between Fishers Island and Napatree Point out into Block Island Sound. Even with this protection, paddlers should be alert in this neighborhood: in the water close to the point, sharp boulders serve as teeth, the tidal currents are tricky and strong, the fishermen onshore and in boats use tall poles and long lines, and the traffic both alongshore and in and out of this harbor is impetuous. All this plus a tall, steep chop! Stonington Point is not a place to dawdle.

East of the point, however, conditions moderate on the way to Edwards Point, and the relatively shallow waters north of the long island called Sandy Point and north of Napatree Point are idyllic. Here is bird life in abundance on the water, on steep sandy beaches, and in the marshes. Powerboat traffic typically is well-behaved and stays within marked channels. The water quality, as far as a paddler can tell, is excellent. The distances are comfortable for a variety of tastes: one can stretch out along the north side of long Sandy Point, actually an island, from beside Edwards Point to Watch Hill Cove for a straight

*Du Bois Beach on the west side of Stonington Point. It might be good to know of this small town beach, for it could serve as an emergency take-out location should the weather act up. There is a traffic pad at the top where a vehicle could be parked while recovering a boat. Under normal circumstances, however, it is only for swimming, and then with a permit.*

sheltered racing leg of around 2 nmi, or nose in and out of crinkles in the saltmeadows' edges, or both.

To cap it off, the Barn Island State Boat Launch (see Fig. 25), with the right facilities in the right place, makes a day excursion on Little Narragansett Bay convenient, easy, safe, and pleasant.

**Fig. 25.** *Barn Island State Boat Launch, Stonington, Connecticut. It appears as little more than a nick in the marsh grass in front of an unbroken wooded backdrop.*

### Shorebirds

The following I tell to birders and others who can paddle silently: the south side of Sandy Point—that long, low, movable bar that reaches from Edwards Point more than a mile toward Napatree Beach—provides habitat for more shorebirds than the northern, landward side. Kayakers can see the shyer, more uncommon shorebirds on the ocean side if they stay at least six or eight boat lengths from the tide line and make no splashes and no abrupt movements, but glide along without a sound. Then the turnstones, oystercatchers, willets, plovers, peeps, yellowlegs, and other species continue foraging and resting as your boat slips past each wave-formed alcove in the shoreline.

## Launching Sites

Note: "CTCAG" after the site name means that a description of the launching site may be found online in the Connecticut Coastal Access Guide. "ConnYak" after the site name means that ConnYak, Connecticut Sea Kayakers, has a brief description of the site on their Web site at www.connyak.org/.

# 5.1   *Bayberry Lane State Boat Launch (CTCAG)*

### Address/Location/Appearance

Bayberry Lane, Groton, CT: 41°19'13.81"N, 72°03'29.71"W. (See Fig. 26.)

**Fig. 26.** *Bayberry Lane State Boat Launch, Groton, Connecticut.*

### Getting There, Parking, and Fees

Route 349 coming south beside the Thames River has been bumpy at times from repairs; the driving directions in *The Connecticut Coastal Access Guide* are preferable when coming south from I-95.

Coming west on I-95 South, take exit 87, which turns off from the left-hand lane. Coming east on I-95 North, exit 87 is a conventional right-hand turnoff. Either way, enter Route 349 south (here called Clarence B. Sharp Highway).

*The Connecticut Coastal Access Guide* directions call for staying on Route 349 as it crosses US Route 1, and continuing for 1.8 miles to where Route 349 diverges by going right on Poquonnock Road; it is 1.02 miles from the Route 1 intersection to the Poqounnock Road intersection. Do not turn, but proceed straight ahead on Brandegee Avenue; 0.57 mile farther on, that street merges with Shennecossett Road, which comes in from the right and gives its name to the road from there south. A right-left dogleg follows quickly, then a 45-degree left turn (to the southeast); 0.6 mile on, follow Shennecossett Road as it bends to the right where Thomas Road enters it from the left (the northeast). Do not be thrown off a little later as Shennecossett Road bends right almost 90 degrees to go from south to west before the junction with Bayberry Lane: it is Jupiter Point Lane that continues straight ahead to the south. Turn left into Bayberry Lane, the next right turn after this curve.

Alternatively, it is possible to turn left off Route 349 onto US Route 1, go 0.97 mile, turn right onto Poquonnock Road, drive to the end (0.44 mile), turn left onto High Rock Road, go about 0.44 mile, and turn left onto Thomas Road, which comes to a T-intersection with Shennecossett Avenue. Turn left onto Shennecossett Avenue and follow it to the intersection with Bayberry Lane, as described above.

There is ample parking for cartop boats and trailers. Fees are charged during the summer season.

### Launching

Kayaks are easily launched at the side of a broad, gentle slope.

*On the Water*

The waterway into which one launches is sheltered from all directions, has boat moorings spaced along it, is about 200 yards wide, and faces the north side of Pine Island and the gap between that and Bushy Island. Traffic is to be expected where the sheltering arms to either side end and the crossing channel begins.

# 5.2 *Peruzotti Boat Launch* (CTCAG)

*Address/Location*

South Road, Groton, CT; 41°20.51'N, 72°02.27'W.

*Getting There, Parking, and Fees*

Route 117 crosses I-95 at exit 88. Come south on Route 117 0.9 mile to its intersection with US Route 1; turn right. After about 0.45 mile, turn left onto South Road. The launch site is before the railroad tracks and about 0.35 mile along South Road.

There is a parking lot. No fees are charged.

*Launching*

Other than the site's location on the small, tidal, and shallow Poquonnock River, there are no particular considerations.

*On the Water*

The current scours out the center of the river both north and south of the railroad bridge, but more than 0.5 mile downstream of the bridge the water becomes progressively shallower toward the mouth, where low-tide depths of 6 inches are typical.

# 5.3    *Bluff Point State Park and Reserve (CTCAG)*

## Address/Location

Depot Road, Groton, CT; 41°20'08.35"N, 72°02'04.56"W.

## Getting There, Parking, and Fees

The site is on the east bank of the Poquonnock River, south of the railroad tracks, and on the west side of the peninsula that forms the Bluff Point Coastal Reserve. It is at the end of an extension of Depot Road, south of the tracks. Depot Road runs south from US Route 1.

If driving west on I-95 South, take exit 88, and at the bottom turn left onto Route 117 heading south. If coming east on I-95 North, also take exit 88, but turn right onto Route 117.

Follow Route 117 about 0.9 mile to US Route 1. Turn right (west) onto US Route 1, go 0.28 mile, and turn left (south) onto Depot Road. Follow Depot Road all the way to the railroad tracks (about 0.35 mile), passing Industrial Boulevard on the left before the tracks, then cross under the tracks to the Bluff Point Wildlife Reserve.

Proceed to the end of this road (0.32 mile), to the parking lot, which is also the trailhead for the footpath around the perimeter of the reserve.

There is ample parking for a dozen or more canoeists and kayakers. No fees are charged.

## Launching

The Poquonnock River's bottom drops off rather quickly beside the parking lot, down to a depth of 7 feet or more, so you will be able to make your way to the narrow opening in the old construction that nearly blocks off the river just downstream.

## On the Water

There are still the shallows at the river's mouth to contend with, so this site is most practical as an access to the Sound itself when the tide is more than a third of the way in.

# 5.4  *Tanglewood Open Space (CTCAG)*

## Address/Location

Seneca Drive, Groton, CT; 41°19.75'N, 72°00.22'W.

## Getting There, Parking, and Fees

From I-95, take exit 88 and get onto Route 117 heading south. Go 0.9 mile and turn left (east) onto US Route 1. Go 0.8 mile and bear right onto Route 215 south toward Groton Long Point (also Groton Long Point Road). Drive about 1.05 miles and turn right onto Brook Street, then go a little over 0.1 mile to Seneca Drive and turn left. Tanglewood Open Space is about 0.15 mile along on the right.

*The Connecticut Coastal Access Guide* has driving directions for those coming west on I-95 South. Following these directions, you'll reach Route 215 by way of exit 89 and West Mystic.

A small parking lot is avilable. No fees are charged

## Launching

This site faces Palmer Cove, which is both tidal and shallow; depths at low tide are less than 1 foot until you're south of the railroad bridge.

## On the Water

Palmer Cove is completely sheltered, with only a single opening beneath the railroad bridge to the south. Beyond that and the roadway bridge beyond, paddlers come out along the east side of Groton Long Point.

# 5.5  *Noank Main Street Dock and Beach (CTCAG)*

### Address/Location/Appearance

Town Dock, Main Street, Noank, CT; 41°19'30.84"N, 71°59' 03.88"W. (See Fig. 23 on page 110.)

### Getting There, Parking, and Fees

*The Connecticut Coastal Access Guide* provides directions from I-95, using exit 88 if eastbound on I-95 North and exit 89 if westbound on I-95 South.

From exit 88, the directions are the same as to the Tanglewood Open Space, up to the intersection of Route 215/Groton Long Point Road with Brook Street: in this case, turn left (to the east), not right. Go 0.3 mile to meet Route 215 again (here, Elm Street); turn right. Go almost 0.3 mile and turn left onto Mosher Avenue, then left onto Main Street. Go to the end.

From exit 89 off I-95, come due south for about 1.15 miles to meet Route 215 (here, Noank Road); this stretch changes names: for 0.1 mile it is Mystic Street, for about 1.1 miles after that it is Allyn Street, and after that, south of US Route 1, it is West Mystic Avenue. Go southwest on Route 215 (here, Noank Road) 1.7 miles and turn left onto Mosher Avenue. The turn off Elm onto Mosher comes before Elm curves right to head southwest beside the railroad bed. Mosher takes you across the tracks and then is met by Ward Avenue on the left; turn right through 60 degrees or so to continue almost due south. Main Street runs nearly east-west; turn left onto it and follow it to the end.

There is space for several cars, but no more. No fees are charged.

### Launching

Use either the dock or the beach at any tide.

*On the Water*

The Mystic River channel is only a few feet from the dock, so be ready for traffic and current at once. Beyond that, go upriver, around Mason Island in either direction, head over toward Stonington, go out to Ram Island, or work from point to point west toward Bluff Point and Bayberry Lane. This is an excellent starting location.

# 5.6  *Mystic River State Boat Launch (CTCAG)*

### Address/Location

River Road, Groton, CT; 41°22.43'N, 71°58.00'W.

### Getting There, Parking, and Fees

This site is on the west bank of the Mystic River north of the I-95 bridge. From either east or west on I-95, take exit 89. You will be trying to get onto Blindless Road, which becomes River Road. Blindless Road, however, is a short (0.2 mile) east-west connector between High Street and River Road, which lies parallel to I-95 on its south side; it only continues as River Road on its eastern end because of a jog in the west riverbank at this point where the river narrows, going upstream. Drive east along Blindless Road, then onto River Road, following it as it bends north and goes beneath I-95; the launching site is on the right, immediately north of I-95. Different maneuvers are called for to find Blindless Road from I-95.

If driving west on I-95 South, take exit 89, turn right at the bottom of the ramp, drive about 0.17 mile, turn sharply right onto Cow Hill Road, pass under I-95, and turn left onto Blindless Road.

If driving east on I-95 North, take exit 89, turn right at the bottom of the ramp, and then almost immediately left at the intersection onto Sandy Hollow Road. Go about 0.35 mile to the intersection with High Street; turn left onto High Street, go 0.1 mile, and turn right onto Blindless Road.

A parking lot is available, and no fees are charged.

### Launching

The Mystic River is from 2 to 4 feet deep at low tide near the I-95 bridge, so this site should be serviceable at any tide. The ramp is steep and in need of repair, but this should not impede canoeists and kayakers.

*On the Water*

The lovely, picturesque waterfronts of Mystic and West Mystic begin about 1 nmi downstream and go on for about 0.5 nmi. The northwest corner of Mason Island, called Pine Point, is about 2 nmi from this launching site.

# 5.7   *Water Street Public Dock and Launching Area (CTCAG)*

### Address/Location

Water Street, West Mystic, CT; 41°21.05'N, 71°58.29'W.

### Getting There, Parking, and Fees

From either east or west driving along I-95, get off at exit 89 and come south on Allyn Street. Turn left at the intersection with US Route 1 (here, West Main Street). After about 140 yards, Route 1 bends left; follow New London Road straight ahead. Turn right onto Route 215 (here, Water Street) about 250 yards on. Keep left at the fork in the road beyond that to stay on Water Street; Route 215 veers right as Noank Road.

The Public Dock and Boat Launch are a little farther along on the left, across the street from Burrows Place.

### Launching

Take usual care in launching into a crowded waterfront and river channel.

### On the Water

As with the Noank Town Dock, this location gives a paddler the choice of the four cardinal directions, all well worth repeated trips.

# 5.8  *Mystic River Dinghy Dock (CTCAG)*

### Address/Location

Holmes Street, Mystic, CT; 41°21.40'N, 71°57.93'W.

### Getting There, Parking, and Fees

If driving on I-95, take exit 90 and come south toward town on Route 27. Turn right on Isham, Oak, or Holmes Street; if on Isham or Oak, turn left onto Bay Street to reach Holmes Street, and there turn right.

The dinghy dock is on the right, across from the foot of Frazier Street. Parking may be available on Holmes or Frazier Streets or on Forsyth Street, the next side street off Holmes.

### Launching

You are launching into a river waterfront that can be busy. However, all craft should be moving slowly, and the current is not a strong factor.

### On the Water

This site is best suited for seeing the sights along the Mystic River, particularly those at the maritime museum, but Mason Island and the Sound are not too far downriver to be added into an easy paddle.

# 5.9   *Foot of Isham Street* (CTCAG)

### Address/Location/Appearance

Isham Street, Mystic, CT; 41°21.51'N, 71°57.92'W. (See Fig. 27.)

**Fig. 27.** *Foot of Isham Street, Mystic, Connecticut.*

### Getting There, Parking, and Fees

Isham Street is a short side street that connects Route 27 (here, Denison Avenue) with the Mystic River; it is north of the East Main Street (US Route 1) bridge across the river in the center of town and south of Mystic Seaport, almost midway between the two. From I-95, take exit 90 and come south on Route 27 past the entrance to Mystic Seaport to Isham Street on the right (west side). If you miss it, Oak Street is the next side street, and Bay Street connects the two along the water.

Parking may be possible farther south along Holmes Street (which Bay Street runs into) or some of its side streets (e.g., Frazier, Forsyth, Church). No fees are charged.

## Launching

The same considerations as at Holmes Street's Mystic River Dinghy Dock apply here.

## On the Water

Again, the same remarks as at the Dinghy Dock apply.

# 5.10 *Williams Beach*

### Address/Location/Appearance

Williams Beach, off Harry Austin Drive, Mystic, CT; 41°20'44.30"N, 71°57'35.62"W. (See Fig. 28.)

**Fig. 28.** *Williams Beach, Mystic, Connecticut.*

### Getting There, Parking, and Fees

Williams Beach is off Harry Austin Drive, which runs northwest off Mason Island Road, which runs south off US Route 1 after it snakes east out of Mystic center and where, as Williams Avenue, it parallels the railroad tracks on the east side of the Pequotsepos Brook.

If coming along I-95, take exit 90 and come south on Route 27 (here, Denison Avenue), then drive east on US Route 1.

Parking is plentiful. No fees are charged.

### Launching

Be careful not to endanger any swimmers at this family beach. The water is shallow offshore, and numerous small craft may be active.

*On the Water*

This is another excellent starting point for trips throughout Fishers Island Sound, but closer in, a paddler may poke around between Mason Island and Andrews and Dodges Islands, investigate Lyddy Island, or trace the convolutions in the shoreline to the west: a creek, the Mystic River, and the intricacies of Beebe Cove behind Sixpenny Island on the way over to the Noank Town Dock.

# 5.11  Barn Island State Boat Launch (CTCAG)

### Address/Location/Appearance

Palmer Neck Road, Stonington, CT; 41°20'14.20"N, 71°52'31.94"W. (See Fig. 25 on page 110.)

*The exceptionally good facilities at the Barn Island State Boat Ramp. This location faces water sheltered by long Sandy Point and one of the most congenial playgrounds for canoes and kayaks along the Connecticut coast.*

### Getting There, Parking, and Fees

The site is reached from the intersection of US Route 1 and Greenhaven Road, midway between the centers of Stonington and Pawcatuck. If driving along I-95, take exit 91. From the west (coming along I-95 North), this exit ramp arrives at North Main Street; cross over and drive 0.3 mile to Farmholme Road on the right. Turn right onto Farmholme and drive 1.8 miles along this downhill, wooded, twisty road to US Route 1. Turn right onto Route 1 and after about 100 yards turn left onto Greenhaven Road. Turn right onto Palmer Neck Road after perhaps 50 yards or less; it is beside mailboxes and appears more like a driveway than a roadway.

Be careful driving along Palmer Neck Road, as it makes a sharp double jog in the middle of an apparent straightaway, which can hide oncoming traffic. Take care, too, where the road crosses over the railroad tracks. People carrying their boats on top of their cars may have an easier drive along Palmer Neck Road than those hauling a trailer.

Drive 0.95 mile from the intersection of US Route 1A and 1 northeast of Stonington to the the Greenhaven Road turnoff. From the intersection of Route 234 and US Route 1 on the west side of Pawcatuck to the same turnoff is 1.82 miles.

## Launching

Rather than use the ramps provided for trailered boats, use the convenient walkway and slip for paddlecraft, which is to the right of the ramp as you face the water.

## On the Water

See the chapter text for the possibilities open to a canoeist or kayaker starting from this extraordinary location.

## CHAPTER 6
# Long Island's North Shore

$T$HE NORTH SHORE of Long Island presents paddling conditions that are the reverse of those along Connecticut's south coast. Connecticut funnels much of the runoff from that state and some of Massachusetts and even farther north into its powerful rivers, but the alongshore waters between the rivers' mouths lie in the lee of the land, sheltered from the prevailing west winds. Long Island's North Shore, however, on average faces north-northwest and so is exposed to some of the region's strongest, most persistent winds; these winds, when out of the northwest, generate waves across a fetch of 12 to 20 nautical miles (nmi) directed at much of the North Shore, so it is no wonder that there are long, broad, and straight sand beaches, some beneath high cliffs with steep, eroded faces that look out across the water.

Nevertheless, there are indentations in the North Shore, almost exclusively along the western half, where the fetch is less. From the mouth of Oyster Bay, the northwest fetch is 7 nmi, and from Matinicock Point not even 4 nmi. As Long Island is a low, narrow terminal moraine essentially devoid of bedrock, it does not collect its runoff into a few strong rivers, but distributes it as seepage into marshes and small brooks. Therefore, the coastal indentations, like Oyster Bay, have no freshwater torrents spilling through them to the sea, just a tidal to and fro. As a result, relaxed paddling is to be found more in the sheltered bays and harbors than along the exposed coast.

Paddlers seeking access to Long Island's North Shore confront two main problems: elbow-to-elbow development of the shore and the

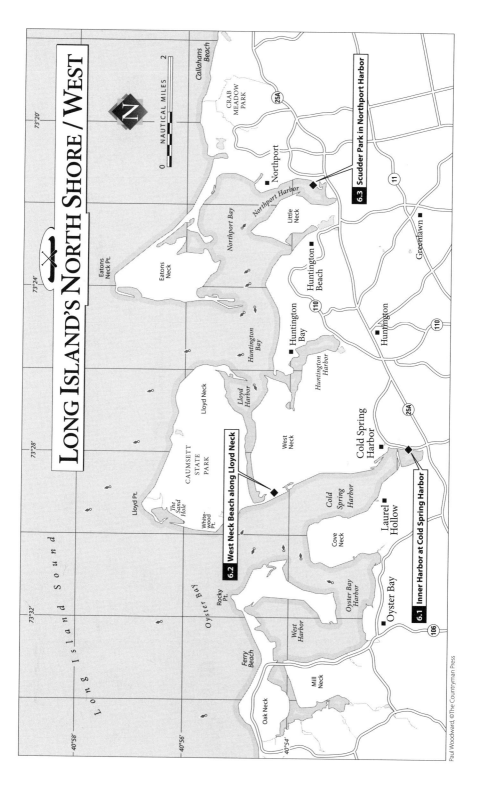

# Long Island's North Shore / West

NAUTICAL MILES

0          2

**N**

Long Island Sound

Callahans Beach

CRAB MEADOW PARK

25A

Northport

Eatons Neck Pt.

Northport Bay

Eatons Neck

Northport Harbor

Little Neck

**6.3  Scudder Park in Northport Harbor**

11

Greenlawn

Huntington Beach

Huntington Beach

Huntington Bay

110

Huntington

110

Lloyd Neck

Lloyd Harbor

Huntington Bay

Huntington Harbor

Lloyd Pt.

The Sand Hole

CAUMSETT STATE PARK

West Neck

White-wood Pt.

**6.2  West Neck Beach along Lloyd Neck**

Cold Spring Harbor

25A

Oyster Bay

Cold Spring Harbor

Cove Neck

Laurel Hollow

**6.1  Inner Harbor at Cold Spring Harbor**

Rocky Pt.

West Harbor

Oyster Bay Harbor

Oyster Bay

106

Ferry Beach

Mill Neck

Oak Neck

73°20'

73°24'

73°28'

73°32'

40°58'

40°56'

40°54'

Paul Woodward, ©The Countryman Press

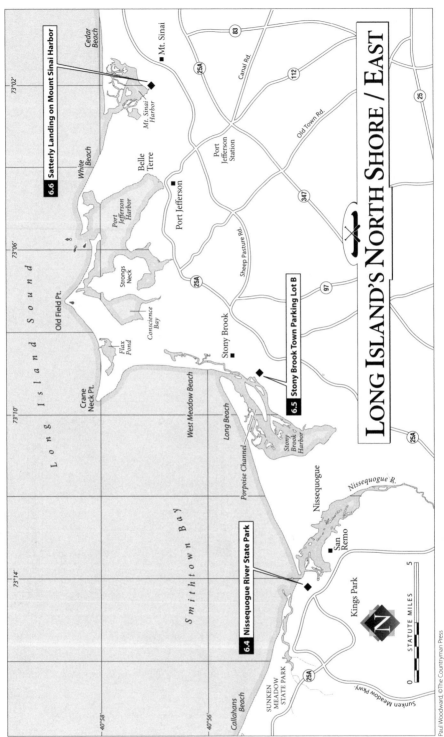

# LONG ISLAND'S NORTH SHORE / EAST

**6.6** Satterly Landing on Mount Sinai Harbor

**6.5** Stony Brook Town Parking Lot B

**6.4** Nissequogue River State Park

Cedar Beach

■ Mt. Sinai

83

25A

112

Canal Rd.

Old Town Rd.

Mt. Sinai Harbor

White Beach

Belle Terre

Port Jefferson Harbor

Port Jefferson Station

Port Jefferson

347

L o n g   I s l a n d   S o u n d

Strongs Neck

Conscience Bay

Old Field Pt.

Flax Pond

Sheep Pasture Rd.

25A

Stony Brook

97

Crane Neck Pt.

West Meadow Beach

Long Beach

Stony Brook Harbor

25A

Porpoise Channel

S m i t h t o w n   B a y

Nissequogue

Nissequogue R.

San Remo

Callahans Beach

SUNKEN MEADOW STATE PARK

Kings Park

25A

Sunken Meadow Pkwy.

73°02'

73°06'

73°10'

73°14'

40°58'

40°56'

**N**

STATUTE MILES

0                    5

Paul Woodward, ©The Countryman Press

absence of an islandwide system of launch facilities for boaters, such as Connecticut has established and maintained.

This chapter describes seven launching sites along the North Shore, from Cold Spring Harbor to Wildwood State Park, all at locations decreed available to the public at large by either state or town. A small number of additional locations, typically where a road ends at the shore, were chanced upon, but all restricted parking to town residents or required permits from the town, not a prohibition against out-of-towners, to be sure, but a distinct inconvenience to the occasional visitor. Port Jefferson Harbor has a launching site open to the public, but as it places a paddler in the company of ponderous ferries, this chapter notes its existence but cannot in good conscience recommend it. An eighth location, one facing Shelter Island east of Southold Bay, is included as well.

*Looking into the western end of the long arm of water behind, that is, south of Lloyd Neck. This is almost directly across the street from West Neck Beach.*

The two westernmost locations in the list of launch sites face west along the 5-mile-long shoreline that runs from the depths of Cold Spring Harbor out to Oyster Bay and the side of Lloyd Neck. Opposite the base of Lloyd Neck is the entrance to Oyster Bay Harbor, which first bends sharply left (to the south) and then curves around to the right so that 4 nmi later its midline points northeast. This final portion, West Harbor, is about 1.5 nmi long and up to 1 nmi wide, where it receives the outflow from Mill Neck Creek and Beaver Lake, themselves constituting a T-shaped appendage with a mile-long stem and a mile-long crosspiece. In all, given a flood tide under a full moon, starting at one side of the mouth of Oyster Bay and going to the opposite bank by paddling along the shoreline, one could have a trip 25 nmi long.

There is wonderful variety along the shore and on the water, too, and places of frank beauty.

Caution and special alertness may be needed in two places: along the active Oyster Bay waterfront on the south side of that harbor and around Plum Point, which forms the north side of that harbor's entrance off of Oyster Bay itself. Plum Point is 1.2 nmi south of the west side of the mouth of Oyster Bay, at the southeast corner of Centre Island; the depths are greater than 3 fathoms close to that sharp point's shore, and the navigational marker red nun buoy #4 is moored close in to shore, so powerboat traffic will be leaving little margin for paddlers rounding the point. The marker for the south side of that harbor's entrance channel, green flasher #5, however, stands a 0.25 mile from the south side of the entrance, Cove Point, the north end of Cove Neck, in barely 2 fathoms of water. Paddlers might be more comfortable entering and leaving Oyster Bay Harbor along its southern shore, then crossing to its northern shore before encountering the busy waterfront.

Huntington Bay is the next large arm of the Sound, which reaches into Long Island's northern shore, going east; it bounds Lloyd Neck on the east and is the western bound of Eaton Neck. From its position between these two necks it extends branches west as Lloyd Harbor, south as Huntington Harbor, and east as Northport Bay, which is as large but not as deep as Huntington Bay itself, being in the lee of

Eaton Neck. Northport Bay, shaped like a camel facing west, stands on Centerport Harbor, its foreleg (to the west) and Northport Harbor, its thicker legs behind (to the east).

*Northport Harbor, seen from Scudder Park. Note the landmark four chimneys peeping over the hill. They are easily visible from the Connecticut shoreline across the Sound from Northport.*

Deep in Northport Harbor, Scudder Park looks north between Bird Island on the left and the Northport waterfront on the right, out along a mile-long sleeve of scenic, sheltered water. Beyond Bluff Point, the west corner of the harbor entrance, Northport Bay opens out to the north (about 0.75 nmi to Asharoken Beach) and to the west (about 2.25 nmi to West Beach, which outlines the camel's muzzle). An exploration along the shoreline of this body of water, peeking into Duck Island Harbor in the north, just forward of the camel's hump, into Price Bend (the camel's topknot), into little Centerport Harbor, and around Bird Island could make a trip of 11 to 14 nmi. All this water is rated benign by *The U.S. Coast Pilot.*

The entrance channel to Northport Bay passes close to the tip of West Beach (just beneath the camel's nose), but it is narrow, nor even 200 yards across; to cross it, set up off the end of the narrow peninsula and paddle a course of 168° magnetic (m) (reciprocal 348°m) for not quite 300 yards to reach red nun #2.

The bottom topography of Northport Bay, incidentally, has inter-esting aspects which may not affect a paddler but are worth noting: 500 yards east of red nun #2, red nun #4 marks the eastern end of shoal ground, with depths as little as 3 feet. Another 500 yards east, red nun #6 is moored in 10 feet of water. Two hundred yards east of that buoy, the bottom has fallen away to deeper than 50 feet, the greatest depth in all of Northport and Huntington Bays, making the camel's forequarters a veritable kettle.

Something, however, that certainly does affect a paddler is the ebb current right beneath the camel's nose. From two to five hours after "Slack: Ebb begins at The Race," (from the NOAA current charts) the ebb current out of Northport Bay runs between 1.5 and 2 knots.

Using Scudder Park as a starting point, a paddler can reach the entrance of Huntington Harbor in 4.25 nmi and be at the end of nav-igable waters deep in Lloyd Harbor after 6 nmi.

Experienced paddlers looking for a trip that takes them out by the Sound itself might consider going from Inner Harbor inside Cold Spring Harbor, out around Lloyd Neck, into Huntington and then Northport Bay, and then up Northport Harbor to Scudder Park, a dis-tance of 12.5 to 14 nmi.

East of Huntington Bay, Eaton Neck, and Asharoken Beach come the landmark stacks of a power plant more than 600 feet tall, followed by Callahan's Beach, and then Sunken Meadow State Park, with acre after acre of parking and access directly to the shore of the Sound.

Leaving the beach at Sunken Meadow to surf kayakers, paddlers looking for a sheltered put-in will be pleased that only 1.5 miles far-ther east is Nissequogue River State Park, with plentiful parking near a dock put there expressly for their use.

The Nissequogue River launching site introduces a kayaker or ca-noeist into a landscape (see Fig. 29) that anyone with a fondness for salt marshes will find enchanting, with twisty channels, little islands, a labyrinth of waterways, and, when one wishes, access to the Sound or, in the other direction, 2 miles of paddling upstream on the surpris-ingly broad but placid river (which is, however, very shallow, particu-larly toward its northern bank).

*Warning sign at the canoe and kayak launching site in Nissequogue State Park. There are other places in the western part of the Sound that could use a similar caution.*

Do take seriously the warning on the sign beside the dock at the state park launching site; it says that the silt on the bottom is so thick and soft that it acts much like quicksand, and this may well be true at other places on the Nissequogue. This is not the setting where one usually thinks about the benefits of a perimeter line on the boat, but clearly it would be better to have one within reach than not, should one sink knee-deep in mud.

If one paddles out the river mouth alongside the narrow dredged channel and then emerges onto the Sound, that same channel extends 0.6 nmi along a heading of 43°m (reciprocal 223°m), accompanied by

**Fig. 29.** *Nissequogue River, San Remo, New York.*

three red flashers and directed toward a red-and-white, midchannel buoy, lettered "NR." Be prepared for sudden changes in wave behavior at the outermost of these three red buoys, for the charts show the bottom at first 4 feet down but slanting away to 40 feet within a distance of about 100 yards. The strong alongshore tidal currents kick in here, too.

This rather unusual bottom topography with its broad shelf (the 1-fathom line lies 0.3 to 0.6 nmi from shore) extends from almost 4 nmi to the west of the Nissequogue River mouth in front of sandy beaches to the hollow at the base of Crane Neck Point 5 nmi to the east of the river mouth. Kayakers comfortable paddling in the zone between surf inshore and greater depths with tidal currents farther out under moderate conditions could range along these 9 miles of the shoreline of Smithtown Bay and, in particular, explore the 4 nmi between the Nissequogue River and the entrance to the Porpoise Channel, which leads into Stony Brook Harbor.

Stony Brook Harbor's (or the Town of Brookhaven's) Public Parking Lot B offers access to miles of clear tidal streams between sandy, shell-covered banks behind sheltering Long Beach (see Fig. 30), a generous public parking lot besides, and Smithtown Bay, part of the true Sound, only 0.5 mile away; this is the facility that offers paddlers the best of northern Long Island.

Walk your boat down to the water in front of the parking lot and push off down the length of the short inlet and then decide: left, right, or straight ahead, and play for hours in an intricate and friendly sanctuary. The speed limit throughout is 5 knots, so wakes and surprise encounters should not be problems. Nothing that a pair of muddy shoes will not overcome prevents a paddler from getting to the water around low tide, but some of the streams between the islets do become narrow, restricting the possibilities for poking around the shoreline. The main channels, however, are always navigable by small craft and, of course, by paddlers.

**Fig. 30.** *View from the bluff above Stony Brook west across Porpoise Channel toward Stony Brook Harbor.*

Paddlers leaving Stony Brook Harbor and proceeding to the right (north) in front of West Meadow Beach toward Crane Neck Point would be well advised to consider the message that a chart conveys: the ebb current at Crane Neck Point flows north, even off the point, and is the fastest ebb current shown along the north coast of Long Island (1.8 knots one and two hours after slack ebb begins at The Race). A kayak, it appears, could make far better progress toward the point than was actually intended, and could in fact be swept out past and around the point, and the paddler could find it difficult to turn around and return, particularly with a west wind blowing.

*The Port Jefferson Town Launching Ramp. It is available, but it is not at all clear that canoes or kayaks ought to be in the narrow waterway as the large ferries, one of which is visible at dockside.*

Past Crane Neck Point comes Old Field Point and then Port Jefferson Harbor, with a perfectly good public launching site west of the ferry docks and with parking and restaurants aplenty, but this book cannot in good conscience recommend that paddlecraft mix with the heavy traffic active there. If the entrance to Point Judith Harbor in Rhode Island with the Block Island ferries churning in and out is bad, Port Jefferson is worse, or at least that is this author's opinion. It seems entirely possible to launch from the public ramp and determinedly stay west of the shipping channel; Setauket Harbor and Conscience Bay provide several miles of waterways extending west and south, wrapping around Strong's Neck, but the temptation to go through the harbor entrance is always there. But, you say, you can always see whether a ferry is entering or leaving, about to squeeze between the rocky jaws of that severe confine. Well, replies the author, that is your decision; just consider, though, the magnitude of the consequences not only for yourself but also the the ferry captain and perhaps his passengers if you get it wrong. There are other places nearby more worth seeing, such as Stony Brook or, just to the east, Mount Sinai Harbor. Also, the flood current through the Port Jefferson Harbor entrance exceeds 3 knots, and the ebb current reaches 2.5 knots or more: these velocities should also act to dissuade a prudent paddler from venturing through this entrance.

Mount Sinai Harbor is a salt pond behind Cedar Beach; it is deeper in its northern third adjacent to the south side of the spit that forms the beach, where two dozen docks protrude like comb teeth from the south side of that sheltering arm. It has low islands in the middle and is shallow in the south, where it becomes a silted-in salt marsh, but one into which kayakers and canoeists can launch from each side of a low, wide wharf and cars can park in the spaces for a dozen vehicles or more.

*The sheltered, almost totally enclosed cove between Satterly Landing and Mount Sinai Harbor.*

This harbor is so sheltered from the Sound that hardly any wave activity can be imagined that could disrupt its placid surface; a tidal current in the angled entrance channel is to be expected, but once inside must dissipate. The fetch across this modest area is so short and the depths in its southern two-thirds so slight that wind would only scuff the water and could not, short of a full gale or more, create waves of any size or power. In short, a kayaker with a strong urge to get out on the water could paddle here in many kinds of weather. Sometimes it is reassuring to have such a place held in reserve for a gusty late-summer day.

Wildwood State Park's beach is 12 nmi east of the entrance to Mount Sinai Harbor but might as well be in another world (see Fig. 31), for there a paddler finds no shelter whatsoever, unless the wind is

*Fig. 31. Wildwood State Park, Wading River, New York. The beach has heavy surf driven by an onshore wind.*

blowing from the south. The beach lies midway between the two ends of the Sound and at its widest point, facing north: if any harsh winds or waves are roaming up, down, or across the Sound, they will surely strike this beach. Nevertheless, determined sea kayakers can add this site to their list of access points along this coast.

In its favor, the beach faces out onto the east shoulder of Herod Point Shoal, so the surf here should be a little milder than it is a couple of miles to the west, where the bottom comes up from 40 feet or more in less than 1 nmi. Two nmi to the east, the shoreline barely pokes out of the general line of the North Shore, yet this is still called a "point."

The shoal water extends 1.4 nmi from shore, but then, near green can #7, plunges to 100 feet and more; there the full effect of the alongshore tidal current will be felt.

## Launching Sites

Note: "CTCAG" after the site name means that a description of the launching site may be found online in the Connecticut Coastal Access Guide. "ConnYak" after the site name means that ConnYak, Connecticut Sea Kayakers, has a brief description of the site on their Web site at www.connyak.org/.

# 6.1   *Inner Harbor at Cold Spring Harbor*

*Address/Location/Appearance*

Harbor Road, Cold Spring Harbor, NY; 40°51'55.8"N, 73°27'45.4"W. (See Fig. 32.)

**Fig. 32.** *Inner Harbor at Cold Spring Harbor, New York.*

*Getting There, Parking, and Fees*

From I-495, take exit 44/45 to get onto Route 11 north (here, Woodbury Road). Continue to Cold Spring Harbor Station, where Route 108 forks to the north and runs due north. Follow Route 108 to where it joins Route 25A; turn right and follow Route 25A north for about 0.5 mile.

Inner Harbor will be on your left. Before you come level with the breakwater, which shields Inner Harbor from Cold Spring Harbor, there will be a small parking lot on your right and a slope down to docks on your left.

Offload on the water side, park in the lot, and launch from the docks or beside them. No fees are charged.

### Launching

It may require some gymnastics to get your boat to the water.

### On the Water

Inner Harbor is sheltered, quiet, and beautiful. Conditions can change drastically when you pass through the opening and head north into Cold Spring Harbor itself and then out to the Sound or Oyster Harbor.

# 6.2  *West Neck Beach along Lloyd Neck*

### Address/Location

West Neck Road, Huntington, NY; 40°54'08.3"N, 73°28'50.1"W.

**Fig. 33.** *Signs at the entrance to West Neck Beach. When driving north towards Lloyd Neck, watch for these signs on the left while negotiating a series of turns. The beach entrance is before them.*

### Getting There, Parking, and Fees

Follow directions to Inner Harbor, above, and continue on Route 25A into the center of Huntington. West Neck Road goes off to the left about 1.8 miles past the Inner Harbor launch site; Woodbury Road (no longer Route 11, however) enters from the right at this intersection.

Follow West Neck Road to where it approaches the shore; it bends right to parallel the beach, and the entrance to West Neck Beach is on the outside of the angle of that turn.

If coming from the east along Route 25A, West Neck Road goes off to the right 0.3 mile after Route 110 crosses Route 25A.

If coming from the south or west, you can reach Route 110 at exit 49 off I-495; that way is less scenic that going by way of Cold Spring Harbor, but is probably shorter.

There is a large parking lot. Out of season, no fees are charged.

## Launching

Launch from the north end of this sandy beach, perhaps in the small creek.

## On the Water

See the chapter narrative for local destinations.

# 6.3   Scudder Park in Northport Harbor

## Address/Location/Appearance

Beach Avenue, Northport, NY; 40°53'36.2"N, 73°21'25.0"W. (See Fig. 33.)

**Fig. 33.** *View north from Scudder Park along Northport Harbor, Northport, New York.*

## Getting There, Parking, and Fees

Here, too, the aim is to get onto Route 25A, but this time in Northport.

If coming from the east or west at the level of I-495 or the Northern State Parkway, exit to come north on Route 231 (Deer Park Avenue), and take exit 51 from I-495. Immediately north of the Northern State Parkway, bear right to follow East Deer Park Road. This merges with Route 25 (here, Jericho Turnpike) and about 0.2 mile beyond the merge, Route 10 goes off to the left. Follow Route 10 up to Northport and turn left on Route 25A (here, Fort Salonga Road).

After 0.4 mile, just before boatyards and before Route 25A heads off beside the water, turn right (north) onto Woodbine Avenue. Turn left onto Beach Avenue, a few hundred yards along. The entrance to Scudder Park is before the end of Beach Avenue, on the left. Go in; the road curves a little and then gives you an opportunity to turn to the right and approach the water.

Coming along Route 25A from the west, Northport appears suddenly; turn left onto Woodbine Avenue immediately after the water and then the boatyards.

There are spaces to park close to the waterfront activity, and others more out of the hustle. No fees are charged.

### Launching

Launch off the sandy beach into the protected waters of Northport Harbor.

### On the Water

Bird Island, a refuge, is directly offshore. The long stocking of Northport Harbor stretches up to the north, where it enters Northport Bay. See the chapter narrative for suggestions.

*Launching site in Scudder Park in Northport. With both beach and floating dock, this site should be usable at all tides. It is used by everything from canoes to cabin cruisers.*

# 6.4  Nissequogue River State Park

### Address/Location/Appearance

St. Johnland Road, San Remo, NY; 40°53'57.2"N, 73°13'49.0"W. (See Fig. 34.)

*Fig. 34. Nissequogue River State Park, San Remo, New York. The dock at the launching site is for canoes and kayaks.*

### Getting There, Parking, and Fees

Again, the launching site is reached from Route 25A, but here to the east of Sunken Meadow State Park and west of the settled portion of San Remo.

Take the Sunken Meadow State Parkway (called the Sagtikos State Parkway at this level) north from I-495, exits 53 and 54. Turn right onto 25A before the entrance to Sunken Meadow State Park. Drive about 1.9 miles; the entrance to Nissequogue River State Park is on the left after a series of rather tight turns, opposite where the view to the right opens out to show large institutional buildings.

If coming west along Route 25A through San Remo, the park entrance is on the right after East 4th Street.

Drive into the park to a small circle; turn right onto a small unpaved road into the woods. The launching site is on the right, not at the end of the woods road.

It's best to park somewhere other than along the woods road, as it is narrow and easily blocked. No fees are charged.

## Launching

Launch from the small dock. The signs convey realistic cautions: "Don't slip," and "Don't step into the mud."

## On the Water

The river is shallow but has 2 or more miles of channel to explore. See the chapter narrative for suggestions.

# 6.5   Stony Brook Town Parking Lot B

### Address/Location/Appearance

Shore Road, Stony Brook, NY; 40°55'11.1"N, 73°09'01.8"W. (See Fig. 35.)

*Fig. 35. Public Parking Lot B, Stony Brook, New York. The inlet here enters the lower left-hand corner of the photo in Fig. 30 (see page 134).*

### Getting There, Parking, and Fees

Route 25A, ever versatile, once again brings you almost to this launching site. About 5 miles along Route 25A west from Jefferson Harbor, that road makes a right-angle turn, to the left as you drive west. At this intersection, Main Street goes right (north) into Stony Brook. After about 0.5 mile, Main Street forks: Shore Road goes left and Christian Avenue, the continuation of Main Street, goes right. Town Parking Lot B is on the left, perhaps 150 yards after the fork.

There are dozens of parking spaces, some shaded, and no fees are charged.

**Fig. 35.** *Watch for these signs to get to the Stony Brook Harbor launching site.*

## Launching

Take your boat to the water directly over the front of the parking lot into a small inlet; if the tide is out, you will have to carry it out to the promontory on the right-hand side.

## On the Water

There are miles of channels navigable at any tide. See the chapter narrative for suggestions.

**Fig. 35.** *The Dolphin Channel leading to the Brookhaven Town Dock.*

# 6.6  *Satterly Landing on Mount Sinai Harbor*

### Address/Location/Appearance

Shore Road East, Mount Sinai, NY; 40°57'11.7"N, 73°01'49.8"W. (See Fig. 36.)

**Fig. 36.** *Satterly Landing, Mount Sinai, New York.*

### Getting There, Parking, and Fees

From the west, driving along I-495, take exit 56 for Route 111 North (here, Wheeler Road); after 1.2 miles, turn left onto Route 454 (here, Veterans' Memorial Highway). After 0.1 mile, bear right onto Route 347; this is the main diagonal that takes you close to Mount Sinai on the north coast.

After 12 miles, turn left onto Crystal Brook Hollow Road and go 0.3 mile to the intersection with Shore Road; turn right onto Shore Road West. Continue on Shore Road West to Shore Road East. Old Post Road enters on the left; drive 0.25 mile beyond the intersection to Satterly Landing on the left, before the road turns right and runs alongside Mount Sinai Harbor.

There are about a dozen parking spaces, and no fee is charged.

*Launching*

Put your boat in beside the low wharves; the water is quite shallow at low tide, however.

*On the Water*

A channel of sorts goes from left to right in front of the wharves, but directly ahead on the other side of the channel are shallow areas and islands. You may have better luck finding a way into deeper water if you go to the right, angling away from the shore, then taking one of two forks that connect to the main part of the harbor; the first is oriented at about 315°m and the second one, the more direct route to the harbor, at about 358°m.

# 6.7 *Wildwood State Park*

### *Address/Location/Appearance*

Hulse Landing Road, Wading River, NY; 40°57'60.0"N, 72°48'00.6"W. (See Fig. 31, page 136.)

### *Getting There, Parking, and Fees*

Route 25A bends south before approaching the entrance to Wildwood State Park; the roadway continues east as Sound Avenue. Hulse Landing Road goes north-northeast from Sound Avenue. The access road to the park diverges to the right opposite 15th and Park Streets on the left.

From the west, Route 46 is probably the best connector between I-495 (at exit 68) and Route 25A; come north to Route 25A, turn right (east) onto Route 25A, continue on Sound Avenue where Route 25A forks right, and look for Hulse Landing Road's intersection with Sound Avenue.

From the east, it is probably most convenient to work north all the way to Sound Avenue, drive west, and then look for Hulse Landing Road.

### *Launching*

There is no way to drive to the water; park in the large lot and wheel your boat down the tarred, steep walkway to the beach. Be certain that you can handle the conditions on the water before attempting to use this site.

### *On the Water*

See the comments in the chapter narrative. There is less energetic water to the left, more energetic to the right, in all probability, and strong alongshore currents beyond the shoal ground. Still, there should be a zone about 500 yards wide in which a competent sea kayaker could cruise along the shore.

# 6.8  Old Main Road by Southold Bay

### Address/Location/Appearance

Old Main Road, Southold, NY; 40°57'56.3"N, 72°48'08.9"W. (See Fig. 37.)

**Fig. 37.** *Wharf beside Old Main Road, Southold, New York, with Shelter Island in the distance.*

### Getting There, Parking, and Fees

Out along Route 25, east of the village of Southold, there is a place where Southold Bay becomes visible to the southeast, and then restaurants and boatyards appear on the right-hand side of the road. Toward the end of this commercial area, Old Main Road veers off to the right, to rejoin Route 25 where the main road bends a little to the right before going over the inlet to Hashamomuck Pond.

Drive in the farther (easternmost) end of this isolated segment of Old Main Road and come back toward the buildings. Park where it seems practicable and launch into the water, either through the shrubbery or beside the first wharf.

### Launching

There do not seem to be any special considerations. However, this is certainly an informal launching site, so ask local permission or not, as your judgment advises.

### On the Water

The land directly offshore, beyond the bar, is Shelter Island. The depths halfway across are scoured out to greater than 90 feet, so expect strong currents. Keeping to the Long Island side of the channel and heading back west toward Southold keeps you in shallower water, almost all the way to Paradise Point. At Paradise Point, however, the current is very strong indeed.

# Glossary

*T*HE GLOSSARY bears down on history and derivations. People have been calling out words that sound like "Starboard!," for example, for well over a thousand years as they, too, struggled against wind and waves.

If one ever needs convincing that the nautical vocabulary of Modern English has deep roots in the Germanic side of the English language's ancestry and in Old Norse in particular, a visit to a small harbor and a stint onboard a sailboat in Scandinavia should prove the point. Northern Germany and the Netherlands also demonstrate the similarities, but there's something about pronunciation in the Nordic countries that instantly sounds familiar. "Boat" is *båt* in Swedish, which sounds the same except for the vowel being a little deeper and longer; it is *Boot* in German, with pronunciation a little closer to the Swedish than the English. Our "ship" in Swedish is *skepp*, in which the "k" is not hard, like ours, but soft, somewhat like a "wh"; try it: It comes out sounding like a windy version of "shep." German has *Schiff*, again, a little farther away from English.

### Boats in General

**bow:** the front end of the boat. The word's origins are unclear, though they appear to stretch all the way back to the Indus River valley and a word meaning "forearm"; think of "elbow." In North Sea sailing ships the grain of the wood in each ship's timber followed the shape of the component; thus, in the keel (defined below) the long, straight section beneath the boat was cut from the straight trunk of a tree, often 60 feet in length, while the upward curving bow and stern sections must have come from a part of a tree either natu-

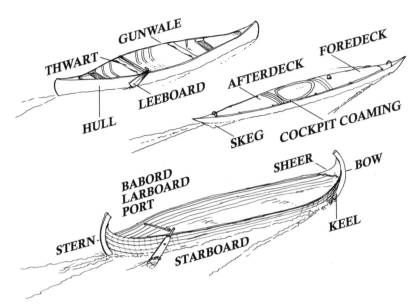

rally or artificially curved, either a "bough" (same root word) or conceivably a trunk or branch that grew while held in a "bowed" position.

**stern:** the back end of the boat. It comes from the Old Norse language word *stjórn*, or the "steering end" of the boat, which is related to the verb *styra*, or "to steer," which gave us "starboard" (see below).

**hull:** a Germanic word; the structural body of a boat, minus masts, seats, and so on. In the case of a canoe, essentially everything that gives it its shape. In the case of a kayak, "hull" is usually considered not to include the deck (defined below), regardless of the deck's contribution to a kayak's structural integrity. The shape of a boat's hull dictates much of its interaction with the water; in fact, you could argue that a boat's hull is that part of the boat that encounters clear water in the normal range of operations.

**keel:** in Old Nordic wooden ships, the sturdy timber that swept down from the bow aft along the bottom of the hull and up to the stern to define the hull's outline from the side. In a rowboat, often a simple strip of wood attached to the outside of a hull along its centerline both stiffens the bottom of the boat and protects it when drawn up on land. If there's a matching strip on the inside of the hull so that the bottom panels or planks of the boat are sandwiched between it and the keel, that piece is the "keelson," which is not derived from "son-of-keel" but "keel-swine" or "keel-pig," another curious moniker for a ship's timber. In a traditional canvas-covered wood canoe with internal ribs to support and shape the hull, the keel was fundamental to its construction; it also protruded below the hull to form a long, shallow ventral fin, which acted to reduce sideslip and to increase tracking. Accessory keels could be added parallel to the main keel but spaced to either side to increase tracking stiffness further. In a kayak, a keel is more a feature of the hull shape than a separate structural element.

**deck:** the surface that covers (most of) the cavity created by the hull. Typically, rowboats lack decks. Kayaks, not considering complications introduced by the sit-on-top variety, are completely decked over, save for cockpit openings to accommodate the paddler or paddlers. In early Nordic boats, the *däck* was removable flooring across the interior of the broad, shallow hull on which the crew walked and under which they stored their cargo and supplies; the removable lath flooring in some old wooden canoes might be considered a vestigial deck.

**coaming:** the raised, reinforced edge around a hatch or cockpit opening to keep out water and provide a rim where a hatch cover or, in the case of a kayak, a spray skirt can be fastened; thus, a kayak cockpit coaming has a lip around the outside edge. Apparently nothing is known about the origin of this term, but I find it suggestive that we call a breaking wave a "comber," sometimes "coamer," and that the crest of a breaking wave in Swedish is *vågkam*, literally the "wave-comb"; the coaming keeps out the "wave-comb."

**babord:** the left side of the boat or ship, looking forward. This is a trick: *Babord* is a Swedish word, not an English word, a combination of "bare" + "board," which is exactly its original meaning. The old wooden ships that sailed the Baltic and North Seas and beyond were built lengthwise of long, overlapping, cleverly shaped, and twisted planks, or "boards" as we might say. The ship's "bord" was the hull's outer sheathing, in particular the part above the water, or the "freeboard." The keel of such a ship swept up at both the bow and the stern in a long, graceful curve, and although on occasion the builders did attach a rudder to the hull's centerline at its curved stern, the shipbuilders far more often attached a large steering oar to the right side of the hull forward of the stern, choosing the right side because, like today, there were more right-handed skippers than left-handed ones. The left side of the hull was bare, "bar" to them, and hence was the "bar-bord" side, shortened to "babord."

**starboard:** the right side of the ship, the one (if you were sailing the North Sea) with the steering oar and thus the "steering-side" of the ship. Even in modern Swedish, "to steer" is *styra*, and to a Swede "starboard" is *styrbord*.

**larboard:** like the Swedish *babord*, the left side of the ship. If you were sailing the North Sea in a wooden ship with a steering oar, you most likely were on some sort of business trip: a little trading, a little plundering, a little more trading. You loaded and unloaded cargo over the side of the ship, probably as it was pulled up against a wharf, and not wanting to damage your steering oar, you placed the nonstarboard side, the bare babord side, against the rocks or pilings; *babord* functionally became the "loading-side." "To load" in Swedish is *ladda*; *ladda-bord* emerges in English as "larboard."

**port:** and again, the left side of the ship. Loading and unloading became more and more to be done in settled ports-of-call for these sea rovers, and the loading-side, or larboard, became also the port-side, as speakers of Romance languages contributed to English nautical terminology. Both terms persisted through the age of sail, but in English "port" has won out in the end, possibly because there's less chance of confusion between "port" and "starboard" than between "larboard" and "starboard" in commands. Swedish has kept the old "babord" and "styrbord" possibly because the "a" and "y" have such distinct sounds.

## Canoes

**gunwale:** in old large wooden ships, the planking covering the heads of the hull timbers where they stood above the deck and on which guns used to be mounted. In a canoe or rowboat, the upper edge of the hull. Pronounced "gunnel" and sometimes spelled that way, too. The "-wale" part came from a word in the Old Norse language for "knuckle," which took on the meaning of "ridge," presumably a lumpy one (the "wale"—used for speaking about corduroy cloth—is the same word).

**thwart:** one of the structural members that lies across the length of the canoe and connects the gunwales. Apparently, the related words "thought," "thaught," "thoft," and "thaft" are or were used in the north of Britain to mean a rower's seat or bench and can be traced back to an Old Norse root.

**athwart:** in the horizontal direction at a right angle to the length of the boat. Also, there's the similar term "abeam," but it's used to describe a position not on the boat; a buoy may come abeam.

**leeboard:** not to be confused with "larboard," a leeboard is a blade that can be lowered into the water on the lee side of a sailing canoe. Because sailing canoes often have a lot of sail for very little hull, they may be heeled far over, with the windward half of the hull nearly out of the water; such vessels need to have their underwater lateral area increased both for stability and to reduce sideslip. A centerboard could be installed, perhaps, but the canoe, when not sailing, would not be a canoe but something else with a tall housing in the center of the loading area: Leeboards allow one to have lateral area on demand without significantly modifying the canoe itself. Each end of a beam fastened thwartwise on top of the gunwales has a blade that can be swung into the water when needed and held in position by friction; that is, there's a port leeboard and a starboard leeboard. A canoe without a sail that found itself in strong winds on open water could benefit from available leeboards; its paddlers could both reduce sideslip and eliminate leecocking and weathercocking by dropping a leeboard from the optimal location along the lee gunwale.

### Kayaks

cockpit: in a kayak, that volume in which a paddler sits. Any kayak used on the bay ought to have a sealed volume in which water cannot enter forward of, and behind, the cockpit; a cockpit must be large enough to keep kayak, paddler, and cargo afloat, even when it is filled with water.

sheer: the upward sweep of the deck, or of the upper profile of a vertical section through the boat, toward the bow and stern. The term "sheer plank" specifies the uppermost plank of a boat's hull sheathing. On old Nordic boats, the sheer plank had a very strong sheer both fore and aft. The sheer of a contemporary kayak is the line of the join between the hull and the deck; this term is preferred to "gunwale." In a wooden kayak, the sheer is set or reinforced by a molding that runs the entire length of the boat along the inside angle of this join, called the "sheer clamp." The fact that the side of the hull makes a vertical and uninterrupted, or sheer, drop from the boat's sheer seems to be regarded as an etymological accident, but the alternative explanations seem no better; it must have been a long, straight, uninterrupted drop from the sheer of an 18th-century ship-of-the-line down to the water.

chine: between the sheer and the keel, the place where the profile of the hull, when seen in cross-section, transitions from vertical to more or less horizontal to meet the keel. The shorter the profile's radius of curvature in this region and the greater the change of direction, the "harder" the chine. The gentler the curve, the wider the angle, the "softer" the chine. Kayaks can have multiple chines, as though fabric were stretched over several longitudinal stringers.

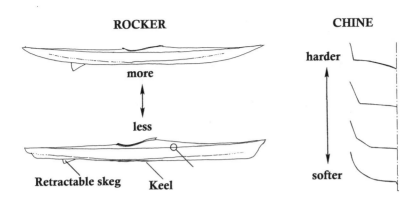

The term may come from the Scandinavian word "kind" (pronounced as something between "shind" and "whind"), which means "cheek," as though the sides of the boat were its cheeks.

skeg: a fillet that continues the mainly horizontal line of the keel to the kayak's stern as the hull itself rises to the waterline. It provides lateral area far back on the boat to improve tracking. The term also denotes a small fin, usually retractable, that can be dropped down through a slot in the keel somewhat forward of the stern and adjusted, ideally, to render the boat neutral in the wind. From the Scandinavian *skägg* (meaning "beard" and possibly originally denoting the considerable lateral area provided all along a Viking boat's length by the part of the keel that protrudes away from the hull planking), a protrusion particularly pronounced at the bow, where it added lateral area that was probably needed to balance the lateral area of the steering oar near the stern. The sense of "protrusion from a keel" remains the same.

rocker: the counterpart of "sheer," as the term describes how the bottom profile of the hull curves up at bow and stern. Imagine the rockers on a rocking chair having the profile of the kayak's keel. The more "rocker" on the boat the less lateral area below the waterline toward the ends of the boat and the less resistance to turning, thus, the greater the kayak's agility, although probably at some cost to tracking.

## Wind, Tide, and Shore

**weather:** the *Oxford English Dictionary* opines that "weather" came long ago from the same Germanic language base that gave us the word "wind." In between we find *weder* in Old English and *ve(th)r* in Old Norse, and you can probably take your pick as to which gave us the modern word. The point is that on the water "weather" means "wind."

### INTO THE WIND

**weather side:** the weather side of the boat is the side the wind is blowing against.

**weather rail:** heard more commonly than "weather side." On a sailboat, the crew might be asked to hike out over the weather rail in order to lessen the tilt, or heel, of the boat away from the wind to improve handling and increase speed or just to keep the boat from going over entirely.

**aweather:** toward the weather side or into the wind. It is rarely used but is a perfectly good word.

**windward, upwind:** "to windward" means "aweather"; "windward" and "upwind" are adjectives, like "weather."

### AWAY FROM THE WIND

**lee:** the most direct ancestor of "lee" is again one of the cultures that sailed the North Sea and the Baltic, as essentially the same word occurs in Old Norse and in German, probably from the northern coast; modern German also uses the word *Schutz* meaning "shield" as in "shielded from the wind," which, like much German technical terminology, is self-explanatory. In Swedish, the word is *lä*, pronounced like our "lay" without the "ee" sound at the end and dragged out a bit.

**alee, to leeward, downwind:** the direction or side of the boat sheltered from the wind. An English speaker at the helm of a Swedish sailboat can say "Helm alee!" and the crew will know what is meant and also think that the skipper has been clever to learn the Swedish word and overlook what they suppose to be his mispronunciation of it.

**lee shore:** the land downwind from the boat, in the boat's lee. It represents a danger particularly to sailboats, which rely solely on the wind for propulsion and is worse yet for square-rigged vessels, which have trouble clawing their way upwind, if indeed they can do it at all. For a paddler, it is a matter of "it depends": It depends on whether the boat and paddler can prevail against the wind, on whether the lee shore would permit a soft landing, and so on. Being in the water beside a capsized kayak a short distance upwind of a rocky lee shore where strong waves are breaking is a ticklish situation.

**in the lee of the land:** where the wind is coming off the land toward the boat, and the land is shielding the boat from the wind's full force. Usually a good place to be.

## A BOAT'S REACTION TO THE WIND

A weathervane is a gadget that pivots to point into the wind, also called a weathercock. British usage substitutes "fane" for "vane." Old Norse had *vani;* modern German has *Fahne,* our "flag." The origins of our verb "to cock" in the sense of "to cock one's head" and "to cock a gun," from the days when you actually pulled back a hammer, seem obscure; the word, however, seems to connote rotation through a certain angle.

That is precisely what happens when a boat weathercocks or leecocks: The boat rotates, or yaws, either into or away from the wind and off the heading you want.

**weathercock:** boat yaws aweather. In other words, with the wind blowing on the boat other than from straight ahead or behind, the boat wants to align itself facing into the wind. Since the bow of

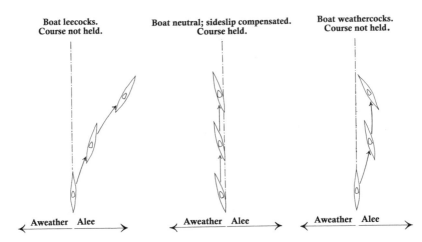

Boat leecocks. Course not held. | Boat neutral; sideslip compensated. Course held. | Boat weathercocks. Course not held.

Aweather  Alee    Aweather  Alee    Aweather  Alee

the boat is not actually managing to move upwind, this happens as the stern of the boat sideslips downwind more than the bow does.

**leecock:** boat yaws alee. The bow sideslips downwind more than the stern, and the boat wants to rotate so as to present its stern to the wind. A kayaker usually finds it easier to compensate for weathercocking than for leecocking; steering involves having a paddle blade in the water behind the cockpit, which adds lateral area at the rear of the boat and reduces the stern's tendency to sideslip still further, so worsening the leecocking.

**(to) heel:** for the boat to tilt toward its starboard or port side. If this is caused by the pressure of the wind coming from the side, then the boat will almost certainly heel so as to lower the lee side and raise the weather side. If the boat is so small that it responds to the slope of a wave, then heeling can be caused also by the boat's hull trying to keep each side equally immersed despite the fact that the water surface is not level. Too much heeling for either reason can cause the boat to assume a more stable position in which the boat is on top and the paddler is on the bottom. Apparently nothing is known about the origin of the word, although it seems it might share the ancient root of "wheel," *hjul* in Swedish, which had the meaning of "to rotate."

# Index